C0-ANO-616

THE
TEN COMMANDMENTS
IN THE
NEW TESTAMENT

THE
TEN COMMANDMENTS
in the
NEW TESTAMENT

John M. McBain

BROADMAN PRESS
Nashville, Tennessee

4281-30
ISBN: 0-8054-8130-3

Dewey Decimal Classification: 222.16
Subject heading: TEN COMMANDMENTS // JESUS
CHRIST—TEACHINGS

Library of Congress Catalog Card Number: 76-19248
Printed in the United States of America

To Dorothy, my wife,
whose encouragement made this writing possible,
and to our sons

Jerry
Dan
Michael

Introduction

In the Ten Commandments are found the great basic principles which underlie the whole structure of human morals and ethics.

They are God-given and, therefore, enduring and permanent. It is unfortunate that many people now look upon them as obsolete and irrelevant.

Some Christians seem to feel that being no longer under "law" but under "grace," the Commandments do not apply to them. It is true that the law was not given as an instrument of salvation, but to reveal to men their own sinfulness in contrast with the holiness of God and therefore to impress upon them their need of the grace of God. In the light of this it would be good for modern-day Christians to consider seriously the high moral and spiritual demands set out in the Ten Commandments.

Jesus expressly stated that he did not come to do away with the law but to raise it to a higher level and give it even deeper significance.

Dr. McBain has made a careful, thorough, scholarly study of the great moral and spiritual requirements reflected in the Commandments and has plainly and forcefully applied them to every area of life in our hectic, confused, irreverent, rebellious age.

Much of our present national and world dilemma grows out of our abandonment of God's Word. The Bible clearly says to us, "God spake all these words." If we are wise we will listen to them!

This book is written in language that the average layman is familiar with. It is readable and challenging. It should call us back to the basics of Christian living.

K. Owen White

Past President
Southern Baptist Convention

Preface

The purpose of these chapters is to help Christians listen as Jesus interprets the Ten Commandments. Too many people have accepted a false idea of separation between the Old and New Testaments. A frequent "proof text" is the statement of Paul "ye are not under law, but under grace." He was not making a distinction between the Old and New Testaments whereby we reject or forget the Old and read only the New. We have one Bible and it includes both Testaments.

Jesus said, "I came not to destroy [the law] but to fulfil [it]." In his own teaching he repeated and interpreted the Ten Commandments along with the law and the prophets.

It is not my intention to press a new legalism on the Christian but to help us all appreciate the whole Bible. Also, we need to see that Jesus did not lower but instead raised the standard for Christians in his application of the law to us who are under grace. He said, "Think not that I am come to destroy the law, or the prophets: I am not come to destroy, but to fulfil. For verily I say unto you, Till heaven and earth pass, one jot or one tittle shall in no wise pass from the law, till all be fulfilled. Whosoever therefore shall break one of these least commandments, and shall teach men so, he shall be called the least in the kingdom of heaven: but whosoever shall do and teach them, the same shall be called great in the kingdom of heaven. For I say unto you, That except your righteousness shall exceed the righteousness of the scribes and Pharisees, ye shall in no case enter into the kingdom of heaven" (Matt. 5:17-20).

It is my prayer that each reader will be led to a closer walk with our Lord by reading these pages.

JOHN M. McBAIN

First Southern Baptist Church
Tucson, Arizona

Contents

1

No Other God

Exodus 20:1-6; Matthew 4:10; 5:17-20; Romans 1:18-24

The Ten Commandments have long been common knowledge throughout the civilized world. They are the unquestioned foundation of our system of rule by law and provide the God-oriented concept of morality for our society.

The Ten Commandments compose the most familiar passage of the Old Testament, but many people may not realize that nine out of the Ten Commandments given by God to Moses are repeated in the New Testament. As we shall see in a later chapter, the single omission is of significance. We will take the first two Commandments together because they are truly inseparable. God commanded, "Thou shalt have no other gods before me. Thou shalt not make unto thee any graven image, or likeness of any thing that is in heaven above, or that is in the earth beneath, or that is in the water under the earth: Thou shalt not bow down thyself to them, nor serve them."

When we come to discuss the matter of the law, we frequently hear a verse of Scripture quoted from Paul's letter to the Romans in which he said, "We are not under law but under grace." I suppose this verse has been quoted more often when we are talking about tithing than about the Ten Commandments. When we begin to talk about man's stewardship of his material possessions, we will take most any verse that will give us relief. Nevertheless, there are some who sincerely believe that we are no longer accountable to God so far as the law is concerned, and they use this text as a proof text. It is true that "a text without its context becomes a pretext." We may be guilty of proving a lot of things by taking verses of Scripture out of their context. As we look at the Ten Commandments especially, and the law as given to Moses in general, we find that most of it is actually repeated in the New Testament, and it's not set aside or denounced or destroyed. The ceremonial laws of Old Testament worship which had to do with sacrifices, especially the sacrifices for the sins of men, were but foreshadows of the real and eternal sacrifice for sin that was made in the person of Christ on Calvary.

The prophecies that spoke of God's deliverance of his people from sin have been fulfilled in the person of Jesus Christ. He fulfilled the purpose of the ceremonial laws. However, as we look at the moral laws of the Old Testament, we find that Jesus has repeated them and has, as Paul said to the Romans, "established them." The standards which Jesus Christ has set up for those who call themselves Christians and followers of Christ are not lower than the standards of the Mosaic law but are in the spirit of the law. We are under grace, but we are not free from God's prohibition against murder or adultery or thievery or false witness. If it was unlawful for a Jew to commit murder under the law, it is certainly unlawful and disgraceful for a Christian to do it under grace. If it was unlawful for a Jew to commit adultery under the law, it would certainly be unlawful and disgraceful for a Christian to do it under grace. If it was unlawful for a Jew to steal under the law, then it is surely unlawful and disgraceful for a Christian to do it under grace. Jesus helps us to see the spiritual reality and purpose of the law as he uses the law as the basis of his teaching. But if we have for one moment thought that we are free to live on a lower moral level than those of the Old Testament, I would remind you of the words of our Lord when he said, "Except your righteousness *exceed* that of the scribes and the Pharisees,

ye shall in no case enter into the kingdom of heaven." Jesus
has raised the standard and not lowered it.

Now let us look at these first two Commandments. The
first one states, "Thou shalt have no other gods before me,"
and the second, "Thou shalt not make unto thee any graven
images, . . . [nor] bow down thyself to them, nor serve them."
We must come first of all to a very factual understanding
of the day and the time in history that this commandment
was uttered by God. The Jewish faith, as we sometimes call
it, or the Old Testament revelation as it might be more
correctly called, was unique during the lifetime of Moses
because it was a religion of one God. There were many reli-
gions of the day—this was not the first one by any means—
because religion is common to man. It has been said that
man is incurably religious. You can go to various parts of
the world and find differences in the culture of people. But
as one philosopher, who was born and lived even before the
days of our Lord, said, "You can find cities without walls
and you can find evidences of the tribes of people without
cities and you can find various descriptions of the ways in
which people lived in different parts of the world, but whether
they lived in stone houses or in tents or whether they lived
in walled cities or in the open plains, you will never find
a culture of a people that was without religion." Man is
incurably religious. So we are not trying to find the origin
of religion, we are trying to find the one true God who should
be worshiped.

One God

Nations of people have believed that there were many gods,
and they worshiped one or another or many. Paul found when
he went to the city of Athens that they were proud of their
intellectual understandings, proud of their philosophers, but
that city at the heart of old Greece had monuments all over
the city to its various gods, for they seemed to have nearly
as many gods as they had population. Paul said to the Athen-
ians that day on Mars Hill, "I perceive that you are very

religious," or as the King James Version puts it, "too supersti-
tious." He noted that they not only had monuments and
temples to various and sundry gods, but even in the midst
of all of the evidence of religion and worship they had a
monument to the "unknown god," evidently in fear that they
might have left one out simply because they had not heard
of him. Paul the missionary began at this point and said,
"He whom you ignorantly worship I declare unto you." So
he began at their ignorance and preached unto them Jesus
Christ. But this is only an example of the plurality of gods
in the paganism of the world.

This revelation is unique in that the Old Testament has
declared that there is only one true and living God. We find
in the Old Testament that his name is Jehovah. Who is this
God who claims to be the only true and living God? We
find in the first book of the Old Testament that he is declared
to be the God who "created the heavens and the earth." This
statement is found in Genesis 1:1. Also in the oldest book
of the Prophets, God is declared to be the God of creation.
As the Creator, he is the greatest God of all gods, if there
were more than one god.

God revealed himself to Moses as the eternal God for he
said in identifying himself, "I am that I am." God is always
spoken of in the present tense when his godly being is men-
tioned. Our God is not the god of the dead but of the living,
declared Jesus (Matt. 22:32). So we come to worship the God
of creation and the eternal "I am," the God who "ever is."
At no point in history is he spoken of in the past tense as
the god "who was," nor need we in our hopefulness speak
of him as a God who "shall be." He is what he is. He always
was what he is and always shall be what he is today for
"he is without even shadow of turning." The eternal God
is the same yesterday, today, and forever. He is the eternal,
living God. He is the *only* living God. He is not to be found
in the dead idols carved by the hands of men. He is not to
be found in the motionless, breathless canvas covered with
paint by the hands of men. Without any semblance in human

figure or in earthly form, our God who is spirit and is wor-shiped in spirit and in truth is the same yesterday, today, and forever.

He is not only the God of love, who is love, but he is also the God of wrath. He is not only the God of mercy but he is also the God of justice. He is not only the God of creation but also the God of destruction when his wrath is poured out upon the sins of men. Our God, who created the earth, as beautiful as the Garden of Eden, as lovely as a home of love, is the same God who created hell for the devil and his angels and created heaven for his own children, as well as his own angels. He is the great eternal God, who is set forth in the Scriptures.

He said, "Thou shalt have no other gods before me." That is, thou shalt not have any other gods except me. He is the only one and he said, "I am a jealous God." It is because of the declaration of the Scriptures, both Old and New Testaments, that we with some peculiarity perhaps, though we are joined in this peculiarity by some other Christians, do not have paintings or carvings of faces, or bodies of people, or animals in our places of worship. We may sometimes use some pictures as visual aids in a teaching scene, but we are always careful to let even the youngest child know that the picture that's used in a Sunday School lesson is but an artist's concept of the person of Jesus.

For Jesus is the only visible form that has ever revealed the person of God, but he was never captured through the shutter of a camera; he was never captured on the canvas of an artist; he has never been fashioned by the carvings of a man who saw Jesus in person. Jesus came that men might see God, and at the close of his thirty-three and a half years on this earth he said, "He that hath seen me hath seen the Father." The revelation of God in person is in Jesus Christ and therefore when we worship Christ, we would, as it were, close our eyes and let the vision of our souls see the love, the grace, the righteousness, and the wrath of God in Christ. We would see the life of God, the eternal God in him who is the same yesterday, today, and forever. We do worship the Christ—not because of the brown hue of his skin or because of the peculiar shape of his nose or because of the height of his stature—but because of the righteousness of his character, the love of his heart, the wisdom of his mind, the truth and unvariableness of his life, and the eternal character of his personality. We worship the Christ, the incarnate God, who took upon himself the form of a servant and lived among men. He demonstrated obedience to the commandments of God and never turned to the left nor to the right from the pathway that was defined for him in the commandments of the eternal God. So we worship God, who "was in Christ reconciling the world unto himself." This is the one God, then, that we proclaim to the world.

In the Sermon on the Mount Jesus said, "No man can serve two masters: for either he will hate the one, and love the other; or else he will hold to the one, and despise the other. Ye cannot serve both God and mammon" (Matt. 6:24). This is indicative of the unchanging character of God as a jealous God (Ex. 20:5).

Paul stated it another way to the Corinthians: "Ye cannot drink the cup of the Lord, and the cup of devils: ye cannot be partakers of the Lord's table, and of the table of devils. Do we provoke the Lord to jealousy?" (1 Cor. 10:21-22).

Jehovah is spoken of repeatedly as the "living God," and also as the one who "created the heavens and the earth." These two attributes, alive and creative, single him out from all other gods, real or imagined. Because he is the living God all other gods being worshiped by men are nonliving or dead idols. The revealed faith of the Bible therefore demands a single allegiance to the one living God that will not bear being shared with another. A divided faith is infidelity, and he will not accept such.

This commandment in the New Testament is found in a clear call of undivided commitment to the one God revealed in his Son, Jesus Christ. Jesus said, "Why call ye me Lord, Lord, and do not the things which I say?" (Luke 6:46), and again, "If ye love me, keep my commandments" (John 14:15). There is no alternate or middle ground. Thus there is no way to ever obey another voice, or give place to another master, or worship another god.

Paul explained it in these words, "We know that an idol is nothing in the world, and that there is none other God but one. For though there be that are called gods, whether in heaven or in earth, (as there be gods many, and lords many,) But to us there is but one God, the Father, of whom are all things, and we in him; and one Lord Jesus Christ, by whom are all things, and we by him" (1 Cor. 8:4-6).

You shall not have any other god before—alongside or in place of—this one true and living God.

No Idols

We must in all honesty to our situation, circumstances, and generation face up to the fact that the possibility of worshiping idols is not a thing of the past. The temptation to worship other gods is not something that died with the older generation in the wilderness of Sinai. Today we must face up to the fact that even some who would call themselves Christians are more guilty of idolatry than they are of true worship. We find in the New Testament some definitions of idolatry that are present today in our own nation.

Paul, in writing to the Corinthians, used the word *idolatry* in reference to the generation of people who stood at the foot of Mount Sinai and waited for Moses to come back with the Ten Commandments. While they waited they persuaded Aaron, Moses' brother, to take their gold, their precious metals, and other possessions and melt them down and make for them a calf. The image was fashioned after those worshiped in Egypt, out of which God had just led them. But when Paul referred to that experience in his letter to the Corinthians, he made no specific mention of the calf, as such, but said to the Corinthians that they ought not to practice idolatry as those in the days of Moses who "sat down to eat and drink, and rose up to play."

Revelry Is Idolatry

Paul also in his other epistles made an occasional mention of the sin of revelry. Let us take these references of the New Testament and declare that in light of the Word of God, *revelry is idolatry*. In his letter to Timothy, Paul said, "She that liveth in pleasure is dead while she liveth." There has never been, in the history of our nation at least, a generation of people quite so bent on being entertained; quite so bent on having their fun at any price; quite so bent on letting life have an outward show of merriment, regardless of the depth of sorrow, remorse, and shame that might rest within the heart on the morrow. Today is a time when revelry is the character of the day. Now there is nothing wrong with being happy, happiness is not idolatry but revelry is idolatry. Revelry is fun for fun's sake, thrills for thrill's sake, kicks for kick's sake. When revelry becomes the object of life and this becomes the evaluation of one's action, then revelry is idolatry. When someone evaluates what others call a worthwhile activity and says, "I don't get any fun out of that," he had best examine his motives for living. Out of every activity that claims our energies and our time are we supposed to have fun for fun's sake? When one is asked for a reason for his actions and says, "Well, I was just wanting to have some fun," does this justify the actions? Even though he may break any one or all of the Ten Commandments in the process, he justifies his actions by saying, "I was just having a little innocent fun." Fun for fun's sake, revelry as the pattern of life, and the objective and the philosophy of life, is idolatry because we, like those before Sinai, sit down to eat and rise up to play. This claims the hours of our days and the energies of our nights.

When revelry in the lives of people takes people away from the house of God, and takes them away from the worship of God, and takes them from the service of God, men are living in sin. Their names may be on a church roll and they may have passed through the waters of baptism and occasionally sit in a pew in a church house, but if they think that the worship service is dull because the preacher is not as colorful as some television personality or that the music is dull because it's not like a popular musical show, then they judge worship by the standards of the world, by the pull of the flesh. Let us judge our own souls; we're worshiping in revelry and not worshiping the true and living God. When the flesh tingles but the soul is dead, when the flesh moves in a secret life of the world then the heart of man is dead in trespasses and sin. That man is in idolatry and under the wrath and the judgment of God. Revelry is idolatry, and it characterizes the lives of many people who today profanely call themselves Christians. God says it's idolatry.

Covetousness Is Idolatry

The apostle Paul, in his letter to the Colossians said, "Covetousness . . . is idolatry." He said it plainly in three short words. Now there seems to be in the minds of some a discussion or a debate as to a definition of covetousness. Is it a sin for a man to want to provide for his family more comfortably, perhaps more luxuriously than he experienced in his own childhood? Is it a sin for a man to want to move into a larger house when more children come along? Is it a sin for a man to want to have a promotion and a better job and a higher rate of income in his middle age than he had in his youth? Is it a sin for a man to want to live on the standard of the society of his neighborhood, of his neighbors? Let us examine our hearts for our motives and our reasons for material provisions, and whether or not they have become the masters of our lives or the tools of our hands.

The Bible says that "godliness . . . is great gain." It also says that we should learn to be content with food and raiment. Covetousness is the greed of soul that shrivels the spirit of a man until he loses the sense of value and integrity of a human life, even his own. Then all things are measured in terms of material value, and materialism becomes his god.

There may be a fine hairline between ambition and covetousness. Covetousness may be determined by whether a man is looking for a larger opportunity to glorify his god or whether he is looking for a more comfortable way of life for the sake of his own self-gratification. Materialism is the god of many people today—trying to "keep up with the Joneses." We are proud that our nation has the highest standard of living of any nation in the world and yet callous to what is now called the pockets of poverty in our country. I remember when America plowed pigs under the ground while men starved to death. There is something to be questioned regarding the materialistic values of our nation when a man places dollar-and-cent values upon his friends and uses them as a means of getting ahead. Covetousness, the greed of the spirit, leaves a man without prayer. It leaves a man with no basis on which to pray and no yearning for prayer except when his material possessions are threatened.

In our prosperity we are most prone to covetousness. It's interesting to realize that in times of economic depression the American people have been more outgoing, and more faithful in their religious practices than at any other time. But let prosperity come and standards of living rise and salaries rise, and the ratio of giving for the causes of God will decline. This is statistically proven. This is covetousness. What is the motive and driving force of a man's life when he will go to work on Monday morning with more of a head-ache than he stayed home for on Sunday morning? He might examine his motives for worship and work. When a man is moved to do some things for money that he would not ordinarily do, though it would be a blessing to somebody else, he can well afford to examine the motives of his life. What does it take to get us to do what is right for the glory of God and the blessing of mankind? Covetousness is idolatry, and God will not accept it. The nation that practices it is heading for a fall. The individual that succumbs to it is heading for destruction, for the wrath of God is upon those who worship other gods and have graven images, though it may be but an eagle or even a buffalo on a coin.

Body Worship Is Idolatry

But there is another form of idolatry. In his letter to the Romans the apostle Paul pointed out that there is idolatry in the camp because "we worship the creature more than the creator." Sometimes we become alarmed at the spread of salacious literature in our country, the publican of pornography, whether it goes through the mails and finds its way to the newsstand or into the comic books or simply on calendars in men's offices. Pornography and many of the practices open for the public eyes of our nation are nothing more than the worship of a human body. And the worship of the creature instead of the Creator is idolatry.

I'll let you be the judge; I'm not a judge—just a fruit inspector. As I have read the multiplicity of articles in magazines, some written for women and some written for men, and some written for the health of both, I have wondered about this health cult we have in our midst. People are forever going on diets—not because they have been told to, for their own good health, you understand. I believe in good health—not as a matter of cult worship—as a matter of common sense for taking care of the only temple of my spirit and God's Spirit that God gave me. I believe in health, but I'm talking about the fad, this thing of folly, of forever trying to lose one more pound than Mary or Bill. I have often wondered about the sacrifices some Christian people have gone through for the sake of fads for body shapes and body weights and yet they have never contemplated making any real sacrifice for the cause of Christ. Have you ever missed a meal in order to be able to give a little more to a missionary offering? In this well-fed country of ours, in which doctors have said we're digging our graves with our own teeth, I am questioning the motives for a lot of things that go on under the name of science and health. It's not because we are really concerned about our health; we're concerned about our appearance. It's that cult of beauty, physical beauty for the sake of physical beauty.

It really is nothing new. You could find the same things in the days of the Greeks. Their art seemed to glory in nakedness. They seemed to worship the human body, and modern preoccupation with sex is nothing but a return to the idolatry and the paganism of the Greeks. What is our worship today? Some people who have lost their modesty in the name of modernity have really lost their worship of God in the name of idolatry. Let's face it. Some of the human nakedness that is portrayed on everything from "Smellyvision from Hellywood" to the bare beaches of the land is nothing more than the flaunting of unlawfulness and disgracefulness on the part of people who want to laugh in the face of God and say, "Look, God, I can put on a striptease and worship my body, and you won't do anything about it." Hell's full of them! Unless you come to worship the resurrected Lord Jesus Christ instead of the body of flesh, you'll burn in hell like it says in chapter 1 of Romans. It says, "God gave them up to the lusts of their own hearts" and that lust is keeping the prayers of some so-called Christian people from ever rising above their heads. It's causing the growth of broken homes in an America that claims to be a Christian nation. It contributes to the highest divorce rate in the world. Why? Because God has given us up to our own lust. It's the idolatry of creature worship, and it's sin. You don't have to take this preacher's word for it. Paul, the apostle, said it. The New Testament is full of it by the inspiration of God. And the wrath of God is against sin and sinners who refuse to repent.

There is hope—there is salvation only through Jesus Christ. America today is guilty of breaking the first two Commandments. James (2:10) declares that if a man is guilty of breaking one commandment, he's guilty of them all. He's a sinner. "All have sinned and come short of the glory of God" and there is no hope outside of the blessed name of Jesus Christ. Jesus said, "Get thee hence, Satan: for it is written, Thou shalt worship the Lord thy God, and him only shalt thou serve" (Matt. 4:10).

2
No Profanity

Exodus 20:7; Matthew 5:33-37

Looking at the Ten Commandments as they are found in Exodus 20, we notice that the first three have to do with the person of God. This is where any true worship must begin—with the person of God. He began by declaring himself to be the only God; secondly, we should not attempt to worship him with graven images or to bow down to any such image. And finally he speaks concerning the holiness of his name; we should not take his name in vain.

The Name of God

It was customary among the Hebrew people not to even speak the name of God because it was held in such awe and holy respect. You and I today are accustomed to reading the name Jehovah, which is a partial translation and partially a transliteration of the Hebrew name Yahweh, which in our King James Version is translated "Lord." If you are accustomed to reading the American Standard Version you will find that the name Jehovah is used to translate the word Jehovah. We use the term "Lord" in English, but I like the feeling of the Hebrew people and their respect for the holiness of the name of God so much that the name Jehovah does not come easily from my lips. They held that name in such high repute, in such holy awe and respect, that it was not to be spoken by human lips, for they thought the very speaking of the name would profane it.

Note the attitude that Isaiah had in the Temple when he saw the exaltation of the Lord and said, "I am a man of unclean lips, and I dwell in the midst of a people of unclean lips." This feeling that above all else his lips needed to be cleansed, was a customary feeling of humility on the part of the sincere and reverent Hebrew. Isaiah spoke profanely because he spoke words in idleness, in carelessness, and sometimes he spoke words that should not have been spoken at all. And so when he saw the holiness of God, one of the first things that came to his mind was the uncleanness of his own lips—he was not even fit to speak the name of God. To say this was an example of the high respect with which the Hebrew people held the name of God, partly at least, due to the commandment that came so early in the Decalogue stating that they were not to use the name of God in vain.

In relation to the general concept of God, Jehovah is the name that speaks of his glory, of his holiness, and of his power. This name was one that described a being that was above all other beings, described a person that was above and beyond all other persons. He was the Creator of the heavens and the earth. He was the one who had his throne high above the earth and was abiding within the holy of holies. This holiness in the concept of God and in the person of God was impressed deeply upon hearts of the Hebrews and you just *did not* speak idly about God. How I wish that our own generation of people could gain this holy respect for the person of God and the name of God.

The Name of Jesus

Then we come over into the New Testament and we find the name of Jesus, which is not unrelated to the name Jehovah. It is the Greek form of the Hebrew name *Joshua* which means "Jehovah saves" and you will remember that the angel announced the prophesied Messiah was to be born of a virgin—"his name [shall be called] Jesus: for he shall save his people from their sins." The concept of salvation was inherent in the name itself, Jesus. The concept of the greatness of

God built into the name of Jesus has carried the concept of the holiness of the name of God over into the holiness and the greatness of the name of Jesus, our Savior. Consequently we have many hymns and gospel songs dealing with the name of Jesus. What a name! Charles Wesley wrote:

> Jesus, the name that calms my fears,
> That bids my sorrows cease;
> 'Tis music in the sinners ears;
> 'Tis life and health and peace.

On and on the hymns have spoken of the greatness of that name, Jesus. Everything that has been associated with the person of Jesus, his kindness, his love, his purity, his compassion, have all been identified with his name. Just to speak the name of Jesus brings to mind the picture of his hands touching blinded eyes, his hands touching deafened ears, his kindness to children when others thought they were nothing but a bother and a hindrance. But he said, "Suffer the little children to come unto me." He was never too busy for people, or too concerned about affairs to become concerned about the affairs of others. He had a world to run but took time to save the people that were in it. All of the kindness, love, and purity of Jesus come to mind by the mere mention of his name. The same was true in the Old Testament for the Hebrew people, because the very mention or reference to the reality of God brought to their minds his great deliverance, the covenant of Abraham, Isaac, and Jacob, the deliverance out of bondage in Egypt, the giving of the Promised Land, the blessing of succeeding generations through Jacob or Israel. All of the greatness of God and his great faithfulness was recalled by merely hearing his name or a reference to his reality. He was God, the Lord God of Israel; and his greatness, his faithfulness, his dependability, his grace, his love, his provision, and his covenants were paraded by Israel's memory when there was a reference to God.

When we stop to think about the greatness of God's name today, or as Christians we think more often in terms of the

name of Jesus, we should recognize all that is involved in
that name. We usually use the word *Jesus* to refer to the
personification of God's incarnation in Bethlehem. We think
of Jesus in terms of the babe of Bethlehem, the man of
Nazareth, the preacher of Galilee, the Savior of the world.
We identify the name of Jesus so much with his earthly
ministry. The name *Christ* comes from the Greek translation
of the Hebrew word "Messiah" and in this concept, the name
brings to mind that as early as the third chapter of the book
of Genesis God promised the deliverer, the Savior for our
world. This Messiah, "the anointed one," finally came in the
person of Jesus.

When we put the two names together, "Jesus Christ," we
have immediately the full picture of the incarnation, the deity,
the crucifixion, the resurrection, the ascension, his interces-
sion, and his return, bound up in what the Bible has related
to his name. Then we come to that familiar expression of
the apostle Paul when he spoke of "our Lord, Jesus Christ,"
which brings to mind that Jesus Christ is not only the Son
of God in glory, or the son of Mary in Bethlehem, or the
Savior of a world on Calvary's cross; but more importantly
we individually identify him as "my Lord and my God," as
Thomas said. Thus we bring him into our own personal
experience and think in terms of our own experience of salvation from sin. He is our Lord and Savior, Jesus Christ. Actually the revelation of God, from Genesis to Revelation and
including our own personal experience with him, is identified
in the wonderful name of our God and our Lord.

Used Lightly Is Profanity

The name of God ought not to be taken in vain. When
the name of God can be spoken and a man lame from his
birth leaps with joy and runs with freedom, then that name
ought not to be spoken unless you are expecting something
to happen. When the name of Jesus Christ can be spoken
and miracles can be worked by the power of the name of
Jesus, then we ought not to use that name lightly. When

we realize that the name of God is identified with him in the creation of the world and in the governing of our universe today, then we should see that the name of God is not used lightly. His name should not be taken in vain for it is a name of power; it is a name of majesty; it is a name with regal authority and power because it speaks of the almighty, the omnipotent, the omnipresent One.

False Vow Is Profanity

There is more than one way to take the name of God in vain; for example, Jesus spoke of this concerning our vows and their relationship to God. In Leviticus we read that his name should not be falsely taken in a vow. We should not use the name of God in an oath that we do not intend to live up to. Taking the name of God in a pledge or a promise or a vow binds our lives unto the death to live up to that vow because we have declared the highest name of heaven as our witness. There are some who say that we ought not to use the name of God in any kind of a vow, that we should not take oaths. I respect their sincerity, and I respect their right to believe as they wish. However, a search would show and declare scriptural record of occasions when the people of God were called upon to take vows in the name of God. One example, in Matthew 26 when the ruler asked Jesus, "I charge you on your oath, in the name of the living God, tell us whether you are the Christ, the Son of God" (Williams), and Jesus declared, "I am the Messiah," he responded to that appeal with an oath that he would take a vow to declare honestly whether or not he was really the Messiah. So Jesus declared his identity under oath, under the pledge of honesty, to be as true in his speech as God is in his reality.

Foy Valentine, in his book *Believe and Behave,* mentions the fact that American people who once were a people of the handshake are now a people of the fine print. He was pointing out that once a man's word was as good as his bond and if he shook hands with you on an agreement, that was it and there were no signatures required, no contracts necessary. But we have gone past that day—a man's word is not necessarily good, his handshake is not necessarily dependable; instead you have to read the fine print of all the contracts to be sure they don't give it to you in the big print and take it away from you in the little print. Where is honesty? Just old-fashioned honesty? Men today take oaths and perjure themselves because there is something basically dishonest about man. This is no surprise. Man has always been basically dishonest. Where the sin comes in is not only in the measure of his dishonesty but also in the fact that he will express his dishonesty under oath because he has no respect for the name of God. There are men who can hardly speak a sentence without taking the name of God in an oath, when there is no occasion for an oath, no need for an oath, no indication for an oath. Yet they speak in the terminology of oaths and take the name of God in vain, and God expressly forbids such usage of his name.

Swearing Is Profanity

Swearing is akin to using God's name in vain in ordinary conversation. While using the name of God, it should not be taken in vain in the sense of false oath and lying under oath. But the name of God is not to be profaned by our use of it even in common conversation. The name of God should be reserved for conversations concerning God. We should speak the Lord's name only when we are speaking about the Lord and should not involve his name in our conversations otherwise. We should speak of "the Lord" when we are speaking about him and not involve his name in our conversation about the weather or something else. We are taking that which is sacred and using it beneath the level of the spiritual, when God asks that his name be reserved for that which is sacred and spiritual. We are not to take God's name and profane it by using it in vain, using the name of God when we have no intentions for something to happen. We hear men using God's name in speaking of the damnation of people and the damnation of things as if they expected

God to suddenly strike somebody dead and damn his soul to hell because they have spoken the name of God in that call for action. God does not so act because of the words of profane men. Nobody is damned to hell because some man condemns him—unless the man who is speaking is to be condemned to hell because he has no reverence for the name of God. The disturbing fact in this matter is that many times we hear professing Christians and church members use the name of God in such a loose manner.

Some of us who would not think of taking the name of God in vain and calling for God to move into action in such a profane manner have become addicted to the use of "slanguage" that is not far from profanity. Did you ever sit down and analyze just what the little four letter word *gosh* really means? It probably was developed as a technique for the weaker, less brave, soul that wants to sound tough without actually using profanity. Well, the intention is there, and watering it down isn't going to change it. I think it's time that Christians clean up their language.

When I was in grade school anybody heard using God's name in vain, or any sort of profanity or vulgar language, on the playground or in school was promptly taken into the washroom and the teacher that heard him would wash out his mouth with soap—literally! I think sometimes that's exactly what should happen today. Not long ago a man used profanity in my hearing and someone said, "You ought to have your mouth washed out with soap" and my mind went back thirty years real quick! It made me wonder if he had had the same teacher I had. I wonder if we as Christians have really stopped to see what Jesus has to say and what the New Testament has to say about taking the name of God in vain.

A False Christian Is Profanity

There is another way in which we can take the name of God in vain and profane it. Sometime ago I heard Billy Graham speaking on this subject when he said, "We take

the name of God in vain when we accept it and allow ourselves
to be called Christians, but do not live godly lives." Do you
realize that the major portion and the real root of the word
Christian is "Christ" and that the name Christian means to
identify us as followers of Christ? His name is being placed
upon us as those who bear the name of Christ. Paul says,
"Let every one that nameth the name of Christ depart from
iniquity." I believe that Billy Graham was right when he
interpreted the Third Commandment to mean that we should
not take the name of God in vain. We should not let it be
placed upon our lives unless we have so yielded ourselves
to the lordship of Christ and have so dedicated our lives to
the will of God that that name can be appropriately placed
upon us as a "little christ." We are followers of Christ.

It is a sin for us to take the name that can call out the
host of heaven with power to answer the prayer of a lowly
saint and speak it loosely on the street in profanity. It is
also a sin for us to take the same name and let it be placed
upon a life that is just as profane as the language of the
profane man that is swearing on the city streets.

God said that when his name was taken in vain he would
not hold us guiltless. Jesus said, "Let your communication
be, Yea, yea; and Nay, nay: for whatsoever is more than
these cometh of evil." James, when he repeated almost verba-
tim the words of our Lord, added: "lest ye fall into condemnation." This ought to remind us that when God first gave that
commandment he said that he who breaks that commandment "shall not be held guiltless." When we take the name
of God in vain it is a sin that demands repentance. It comes
to evil; it brings condemnation; it brings guilt upon us for
we have broken a commandment of God and we have profaned
the sacred name of the eternal God.

We can turn to the New Testament again and find for
example in Acts 5 the record of Ananias and Sapphira. I have
often wondered why there is only one record of it. I am sure
that it wasn't the only time it ever happened. That was a
couple that saw the potential for pride and prestige in some

other people who were making sacrificial offerings. They were selling their houses and land and putting the full price of it into the treasury of the church and they were becoming leaders—not because of their money but because of their dedication. But people whose hearts are not right with God can't tell the difference between a dollar and a dedication.

Barnabas and some of the others were filled with faith and grace and the Spirit of the Lord and their lives were dedicated to God, so that their possessions meant nothing to them unless they could use them for the glory of God. Ananias and Sapphira thought they could get the same kind of prestige and assume the same places of leadership if they gave as much money as Barnabas did. So they sold their property but kept back part of the money which they brought before the church. Peter asked Ananias, "Did you sell your farm for so much?" He said yes. Peter said, "You just got through lying to God," and Ananias dropped dead right there. They took him out and buried him. In a little while his wife showed up, and Peter said to her, "Sapphira, your husband left this money here. Is this the full price of the farm?" When she said yes, Peter said, "You are lying, too," and she dropped dead right there. I don't know whether they stood up and gave a vocal pledge or signed a card, but Peter knew what kind of promise they had made, and apparently Peter knew they promised to give it *all*. But they lied to God and God will not hold them guiltless who make false vows in his presence, and to his church.

I think there have been a lot of false vows made under the name of God. They haven't all had to do with pledge cards, and they haven't all had to do with the giving of money. More of them have had to do with the giving of life. How glibly we sing "I Surrender All" when we don't mean to surrender at all. We will surrender all that he takes away from us. We do not mean to voluntarily give it at all. But we make promises when we sing invitation hymns, and we sing dedication hymns as if they meant nothing. I believe that one of the reasons there are not many souls saved during the invitation time in a Baptist church is because we're singing songs of dedication and decision that are not coming from the heart. We have no intentions of doing what that song says, any more than Ananias intended to give the full price of his farm to the church. Is it any wonder that our prayers are unanswered? Is it any wonder that our baptistries rust out in many churches? Could it be that while they were singing the same old songs of Zion and making the same old promises of the saints and singing the same old songs of the church, they did it with empty hearts? They took the name of God in vain in his dedicated house. As the Scripture says, "It is a fearful thing to fall into the hands of the living God."

In Romans, (1:30-32) Paul listed "backbiters, haters of God, despiteful, proud, boasters, inventers of evil things, disobedient to parents, without understanding, covenantbreakers, [and I think that includes church covenants], without natural affection, implacable, unmerciful: who knowing the judgment of God, that they which commit such things are worthy of death, not only do the same, but have pleasure in them that do them." When Jesus was asked to teach the disciples to pray, the first thing he taught them to say was, "Hallowed be thy name." May his name be holy on our lips and in our lives. Truly, we take God's name in vain when we let it be applied to us without living the life that goes with it. This includes our attitudes and our speech.

3
The Lord's Day

Exodus 20:8-11; Mark 2:23 to 3:6

Earlier I stated that one of the Ten Commandments was not repeated in the New Testament. This fact, I believe, is significant. Nine out of the ten are repeated almost word for word in the New Testament. However, the commandment concerning the sabbath is not repeated as a commandment. Rather, we find references to the sabbath in the ministry of our Lord, such as the time when he was criticized for not keeping the sabbath as it was interpreted in his day.

The Pharisees had many commandments, most of which were traditions of the fathers, as Jesus called them. He also called them "man's traditions." All sorts of commandments and interpretations of commandments limited the things that a man could do and could not do. Strict restrictions were enforced on the distance you could walk on the sabbath day. I suppose they had some rather heated arguments as to whether or not one ought to eat an egg that had been laid on the sabbath day because the hen worked at laying it. As ridiculous as this sounds, a little study and research on the traditions of that day will show that they were just that bad. On the other hand, Jesus gave a very practical interpretation of this commandment. But before we come to the New Testament interpretation, we need to have a little deeper and broader appreciation for what the sabbath was, as God himself established it in the Old Testament, and particularly in the tablet of ten.

The History of the Sabbath

We note, for example, that the observance of the sabbath did not begin with the Ten Commandments. This is something we sometimes overlook in our haste to find an escape from the teachings of God. We find it so easy to say, "Well, that pertains to the law, and as Christians we are not under law; we are under grace." The man that doesn't want to tithe uses that excuse, and the man that doesn't want to observe one day a week for the glory of God will use the same excuse. The fact of the matter is, both of the practices are older than the Ten Commandments. The observance of the sabbath goes back to creation itself, God created the world in six days and rested on the seventh. The Hebrew word *sabaton* which is translated *sabbath* in our English Bible is a word which means "rest." It is a special period that is reserved and called "the rest" and the seventh day was the day of "the rest." It was the day in which God rested from his labors of creation.

From that day till this, God has always intended that his people follow his example. The more godly (Godlike) a man is, the easier it is to acknowledge him as a man of God. The people of God are to be known by their fruits—they are to be observed by external evidences of following the practices of God. This is not what makes a man a man of God. The practices of God's people do not make them God's people, but they are the simplest way of identifying God's people because God's people do practice the ways of God. When God gave the Commandments it was clear that his objective was the disciplining of his people so they would become Godlike in their lives. This is God's purpose for you and me. In the book of Romans, (8:29), we are told that God planned ahead of time—those "whom he did foreknow, he also did predestinate to be conformed to the image of his Son." We are to be Christlike. That is one of the reasons he redeemed us—because the unredeemed man is not Christlike. And so, as we go back into the Old Testament as well as in the New, we find this developing pattern for God's people: they practice what God practices, learn to do God's will, learn to think as he thinks, learn to love what God loves, and learn to hate what God hates. In this pattern God made the world in six days and rested on the seventh. Surely, a person can make a living in six days and rest on the seventh. This is the background of the day. It originated in God's own pattern. The Scripture says, "God blessed the seventh day, and sanctified it." It is a holy day.

Those who have preceded us set the pace perhaps, but the problem with our generation has been an increasing determination to make a holiday of the sabbath instead of a holy day. God made it a holy day—not a holiday. The sabbath was a special day in religious observance. We, with our New Testament orientation, have come to think of the sabbath as just one day a week, but if you will study your Old Testament, you will find that the weekly sabbath was only one of many. Likewise, we have thought of tithing as the first tenth of all the increase, but that was just the first tithe. The Old Testament indicates that the Jews observed at least three tithes. The Christian who thinks he is doing something big by tithing is getting off easy. The Jews had their weekly sabbath, their monthly sabbath, and an annual sabbath; such as, the day of atonement, the Passover, and other special occasions that came once a year. These were holy days that were observed, and work was forbidden as on the weekly sabbath. These were days in which various things were commemorated. The atonement, for example, commemorated God's gracious forgiveness of sin. The Passover commemorated God's gracious deliverance out of the bondage of Egypt. And so with these various sabbaths, they were always remembering something of special importance to them. It was a day of remembrance. Likewise, the weekly sabbath was a day of remembrance of God's creation.

There were some other sabbaths. There was the sabbath of the land, for example. We in America think we have done something great in recent years. When our national government first began to develop the soil conservation program, my preacher-father expressed on several occasions, "If the people of America would just go back to the Bible and treat the soil as God said to treat the soil, we wouldn't have the problems that demand soil conservation today." You see the Bible teaches the stewardship of the soil, and every farmer needs to take note that the soil belongs to God. You are just a gardener, that's all. The stewardship of the soil acknowledges the lordship of the Lord, our God.

The sabbath of the soil required that every seventh year the land would lay idle. Modern government came along and talked about letting certain land lie idle and started teaching crop rotation, ideas which may be found in the Old Testament. God prescribed it centuries ago. But because God's people forgot the sabbath days (notice the plural), they forgot the stewardship of the soil. God took those people off the soil and let them go into the captivity of Babylon for how many years? Seventy of them. You will find that the Bible expressly says that this was "that the soil might have its sabbath." They had desecrated the soil because they ignored God's commands for the conservation of it. So our whole universe is geared to sabbaths, including the soil.

Some years ago I read the statement of a physicist who declared that by scientific experiment it had been proven that even the material things of the world have been so created that by their very nature they are geared to a six-day week. He said that even machinery checked for the total number of hours that it will operate, from the day of its manufacture to the day that it breaks down, will have more hours of actual service if it is allowed to rest one day a week than if it is operated seven days a week. As a matter of scientific evidence, he says, this was proven to be so. This ought not to be new to us. God said the soil would produce better if it were allowed to rest one-seventh of the time. It should be no surprise to us then that that which comes out of the soil, the minerals that may be fashioned in the machinery, shall have built within them the nature that is within the soil from which they came—that one-seventh of the time is geared to rest.

Should man be any different? He likewise came from the earth, and God has so created us that our lives are geared to a six-day week.

American leaders today are talking about a four-day work-week. They have built the five-day week into our economy and now they want to go to a four-day week. And some want a three-day week to see if they can solve the problem of unemployment. Well, it may solve the problems of unemployment, but it's sure going to ruin us Christians! The recent development of three-day weekends for certain holidays has been no boon for the churches. If it were a weekly arrangement, many would lose their religion completely. If we had another day so we really had a long weekend every week, we would just simply lose our religion. We would lose our sense of God.

God set into the very nature of our world a period of rest for man, for soil, for machinery, for all of the world, and to live any other way is to defy the laws of nature and to destroy ourselves.

God also built into nature, as you'll find in the Old Testament, the value of property. The soil was geared to the sabbath because every seventh year the soil was to be left idle. Every fiftieth year was a Jubilee year, the soil got an extra sabbath, not only that, but also on the fiftieth year, the Jubilee year, all of the soil returned to its original owner. You did not add land to land and houses to houses, which the Bible forbids as a matter of grasping greed, because every time you sold a piece of land you not only evaluated it according to its productivity and fertility, but you also priced it according to the number of years left before the Jubilee year. If you were at the twenty-five-year point, the land was worth only half as much as it would have been at the beginning because you could only hold it half as long. This provided for the poor that may have lost their inheritance. They always could look forward to the Jubilee year for which God had made preparations. God provides for the poor. God has provided for the health of mankind, and so we find built into this really not the fact that God wanted one day out of seven to be observed for the sake of the days, but as Jesus said, "for the sake of the man." God did not make man in order to have somebody to observe the sabbath. He made the sabbath for the blessing of man.

Reasons for the Sabbath

Now then, what are the real reasons underlying the need for the sabbath? In the first place, we find it expressly stated in the books of Leviticus and Deuteronomy that the sabbath was observed by man as a remembrance of his covenant with God. Also, the prophet Ezekiel declared this as a testimony of his covenant. In this covenant people declared their allegiance to God by their observance of the sabbath because the sabbath was God's day, and God's people observed it. The pagan nations ignored the sabbath. The heathen around them and within their nation did not observe it, but God's people observed the sabbath. This was a distinctive part of their testimony. It is today, also, a part of our testimony that we are God's people. It was and still is, a part of the covenant God's people have with God.

And then God said that it was a testimony of their deliverance. He wanted them always to remember that it was the Lord God who delivered them out of Egypt. This came as a new significance revealed in the book of Deuteronomy. Up to this point the emphasis had been on God, their Creator. God created the world in six days and rested the seventh. You, as God's people, recognize God as your Creator, the Creator of the heavens and the earth, and since you are his people you should observe a day of rest as he does. But Deuteronomy added a flavor to the sabbath for the Israelites were also to remember on that day that it was God who delivered them out of bondage.

An interesting story was published a few years ago. A church in one of the southern states, faced with the problem of expansion, was confronted with the problem of adequate parking space. Nearby was a large supermarket that had ample parking space which was not used on Sunday. Being a religious community, their department stores, grocery stores, and business houses were closed on Sunday. The church secured from the supermarket permission to use its parking lot. However, the owner of the parking facility said that he would like to have the agreement in writing because there was one stipulation he wanted to make. He wanted it recorded so they would never forget this one stipulation. The contract stated that the church could use the parking lot on only fifty-one Sundays a year. One Sunday out of the year had to be designated as a "no parking" Sunday. He said, "For fifty-one Sundays, I make no charge. I give it to you free. But on one day a year I want you to remember who gave it to you."

In a similar way God says, "I give you the soil; I have made you the caretaker of my garden, and you can eat of the fruit of the garden. All of the beasts of the field and the fowl of the air shall likewise be yours as meat to eat. Here is the world; have dominion over all of it, but *one day a week* you just sit down and remember who gave it to you." Do you see why it is that God set a day into the nature of the universe, in which the God of the universe is to be acknowledged and remembered?

As we come into the New Testament, what do we find? We find in the Gospels that Jesus was frequently criticized for disregarding the sabbath day. He walked with his disciples on the sabbath day, but the Pharisees didn't criticize him for walking too far. In the law of the Old Testament it was permitted that a traveler passing by a grain field could take enough grain to meet his immediate needs. He could not carry it off—he had to eat it on the spot. But passing by a grain field, he could take the grain and work it in his hands and separate the grain from the chaff. I have had the privilege of doing this in a good old-fashioned American wheat field. You just roll it in your hands until you have separated the chaff from the grain and then blow the chaff from the palm of your hand and chew the wheat. It tastes real good. It's nourishing because it is the whole grain and has not been bleached, boiled, and milled so much as to lose its goodness.

The common practice of the day of our Lord was to take a handful of the grain from the field and roll, separate and eat it. Even though the Old Testament Mosaic law said the stranger was entitled to grain from your field, the Pharisees said, "No, no, not on the sabbath day, because you're harvesting wheat and you're threshing on the sabbath. That's work." Just one handful, but it's work. You were considered a gracious host to feed the stranger as he passed by. You planted by the field for his provisions, just as when you cut the grain in the field, the grain in the corners of the fence rows was left there for the poor to thresh for themselves; so the farmer took care of the poor and the stranger by the way he performed his stewardship of the soil.

Jesus was criticized once because his disciples fed themselves this way on a sabbath. He responded that God was more concerned about the *man* than he was the *day*. Likewise, Jesus healed on the sabbath day and they criticized him for this because it was an act of work for the man to stretch forth his hand in response to Jesus' command. Jesus placed his hand on a sick body or on blinded eyes, and they criticized him for doing the work of a physician on the sabbath day. Jesus pronounced an interpretation of this commandment that stands to this day when he said, "The sabbath was made for man, and not man for the sabbath."

The Day of the Sabbath

Just as Moses in the book of Deuteronomy added to the significance of the seventh day, the sabbath of God, we find some new significance in the New Testament.

Jesus went into the synagogue on the sabbath day—"as his custom was"—and he brought up his disciples in the same tradition. The tradition changed when our Lord was crucified on the cross outside the walls of Jerusalem and was buried in the tomb and on the third day arose from the dead. That third day happened to be the first day of the week—not the seventh. I suppose we might strain a point in saying that Jesus did his work of redemption on Friday and rested in the tomb on Saturday, the sabbath day, and arose on the first day of the week. God created man on the sixth day and rested. God in Christ redeemed man on the sixth day, rested in the tomb on the seventh day and arose from the dead on Sunday, the first day. But the significance we note is that from the day of the resurrection on through the remainder of the New Testament, we find the pattern of Christians worshiping on the *first* day of the week.

The name "the Lord's Day" is given to this day in Revelation 1:10. We have the revelation of Jesus to John on the Isle of Patmos and John says, "I was in the Spirit on the Lord's Day." We believe in the pattern of the Christians of the New Testament that John was referring to the first day of the week, that was uniquely "The Lord's Day," because it was the day in which Christians assembled themselves together to remember the same things that the Jews had remembered on the seventh day. They remembered the Creator. Christians remember the Creator for it's the same God they worship. Jews remember their deliverance out of bondage in Egypt by commemorating it on the seventh day and on the Passover day. Christians commemorate their deliverance from the bondage of sin by assembling themselves on the Lord's Day, on this holy day. Likewise, on Easter Sunday we have the annual observance of our remembrance of the deliverance we have because of the resurrection of Jesus Christ, our risen, wonderful Lord. He is our Savior and on the Lord's Day we worship a risen Lord! The significance of the Creator, the significance of our deliverer, the significance of our provider, are all bound up in our observance, also.

He has not changed the meaning, but he has changed the day because there is a change. As the New Testament tells us in the book of Hebrews (8:13), when there came a "new covenant," we then had an old covenant. When we found ourselves with a new day, there was an old day. Christians

are the people of God of a new day, which comes in the new
covenant, and is greater than the promises of the old covenant
because we have a Christ, a Savior, who the Scripture says
in Hebrews is "worthy of more glory than Moses." He has
a name that is better than the angels. He has a covenant
that is better than the old. He has promises that are better
than the old. He has a sacrifice that is better than the old,
for the perfect sacrifice is the person of Jesus Christ, our
risen Redeemer, and we worship him on the Lord's Day.

The Jew worships on the seventh day to commemorate
God's act in creation. The Christian worships on the first
day, the Lord's Day, to commemorate God's act of redemption
(re-creation, 2 Cor. 5:17).

In the New Testament the Christians were gathered together on the first day of the week. This was true on the
very day our Lord arose from the dead. Christians were
assembled together in the early morning hours of that first
day of the week when the women came to tell them that
Jesus had risen from the dead. The women were a little late
for worship that morning perhaps, because they came by way
of the tomb. And then, we notice that on the first Sunday
night of the resurrection day, they were assembled again in
the evening hour, and they were all there but Thomas. I
wonder what would happen today if on the Lord's Day night,
as we looked at the congregation gathered together in a
dedicated place for worship, only one out of every eleven
members was absent. What would happen? What would happen to your church's activities on the Lord's Day if suddenly
we became New Testament disciples and were at church at
the hours of assembly as a part of the day's schedule?

Again, I have often wondered what would happen to the
life of a church if the ten out of the eleven busied themselves
in the next seven days to find that one out of eleven and
see that he was present on the next Lord's Day. After all,
one week after the resurrection they were *all* present. What
a day of rejoicing that would be! I remind you that it says
in the Word of God in the New Testament: "Not forsaking

the assembling of ourselves together, as the manner of some is." Even in the first century some had developed the habit of forsaking the assembly, and the New Testament gives as a commandment to God's people, "not forsaking the assembling of ourselves together, as the manner of some is."

By the grace of God we need to provide for ourselves the spiritual food and strength needed for the coming week and that's what worship is for on the Lord's Day. Some have joked with me about it since I made this statement some years ago, but I repeat it anyway. Do you know why it is that some people come to church only on Sunday morning? For the same reason that I do not eat hot cakes often for breakfast. I'm not accustomed to that kind of breakfast. I don't usually do enough physical labor in a day's time to justify that kind of breakfast, and I rather have the feeling that some people take in only one worship service a week because that's about all they intend to do anything about anyway. If you were going to do all that God intended for you to do this week, you would need a full hour on Sunday morning with no consciousness of the arrival of twelve o'clock. You would need another full hour or two on Sunday night and another hour on Wednesday night. You'd come in weak and worn out on Wednesday night and say, "Preacher, pray to God that I get filled up again so I can make it until Sunday; I'm spiritually empty." When your soul is sick, and you're in need of the Word and the nourishments of God's Word, you need to find God and worship. This is what it's all about.

I wish that we all would dedicate our lives anew to God and let our observance of the Lord's Day be the declaration that God is our God. Let it be the remembrance of God's deliverance of your soul from the bondage of sin, let it be the declaration that you are a man of God, and let it be the hunger of your heart to be fed, to be "in the Spirit of the Lord on the Lord's Day."

4
Honoring Our Parents

Exodus 20:12; Matthew 15:1-9; Ephesians 6:1-4

"Honor thy father and thy mother: that thy days may be long upon the land which the Lord thy God giveth thee." Turning to the New Testament, the Gospel of Matthew 15:1-9, reads, "Then came to Jesus scribes and Pharisees, which were of Jerusalem, saying, Why do thy disciples transgress the tradition of the elders? for they wash not their hands when they eat bread. But he answered and said unto them, Why do ye also transgress the commandment of God by your tradition? For God commanded, saying, Honour thy father and mother: and, He that curseth father or mother, let him die the death. But ye say, Whosoever shall say to his father or his mother, It is a gift, by whatsoever thou mightest be profited by me: And honour not his father or his mother, he shall be free. Thus have ye made the commandment of God of none effect by your tradition. Ye hypocrites, well did Esaias prophesy of you, saying, This people draweth nigh unto me with their mouth, and honoureth me with their lips; but their heart is far from me. But in vain they do worship me, teaching for doctrines the commandments of men."

There is another passage in Paul's letter to the Ephesians 6:1-4, "Children, obey your parents in the Lord: for this is right. Honour thy father and mother; which is the first commandment with promise; That it may be well with thee, and thou mayest live long on the earth. And, ye fathers, provoke

not your children to wrath: but bring them up in the nurture
and admonition of the Lord."

Tribute to Mothers

At least annually we show honor and blessing to our
mothers.

For the sake of your mother and for the sake of being honest
in the knowledge and memory of my mother, I certainly want
by way of introduction to this chapter to pay a very brief
tribute to mothers. I'm not sure that our mothers appreciate
all of the things we say—not because they do not want to
be honored—but some of them, being the humble mothers
that they are, are embarrassed by kind words, especially on
Mother's Day. If we would say them more often they might
become more accustomed to them. Also I have gathered the
impression from some of them that some of the nice and
glorious things that are said about mothers, especially by
preachers, leave them in a rather embarrassing position because it sets a standard they are expected to live up to
throughout the year. We have great respect for our mothers.
It has been traditional, and I presume greatly true, that the
moral standards of a nation are set by the mothers.

It is a proverb of an earlier generation that "the hand that
rocks the cradle rules the world." These ideas may be a bit
philosophical, they may be a bit perfectionist, or idealist, but
there is a great deal of truth there because the character
and the commitment of our mothers has had a most profound
effect upon our lives for good, as well as occasionally perhaps
for evil. It has been said that "behind the life of every success-
ful man is at least one woman." Usually at least two, I think,
his wife and his mother. These two women have frequently
been the secret between success and failure for a man who
might otherwise have wavered. A mother's or wife's own dedication is an inspiration. Her own character is a pattern for
her children as well as her husband.

Our homes, dominated by the presence of the mother more
hours of the day than by the father, many times are the

reflection of the mother, though it is possibly true that that reflection is often distorted when dad walks in. Our homes are greatly determined by the character of the parents. Those tender years of childhood are the most formative years of the mind and character of the youth. We give a great deal of credit and sometimes a great deal of blame to our public schools for the outcome of our children. But we must remember that parents have had their children for the first and most important five or six years before the school has a chance. From the responsibilities of parenthood comes glory for the parents because fortunately we have more successes than failures, or else our world would have long since fallen away.

The Plan of the Home

The plan for the home described in the Scripture includes the fathers with the mothers, because the text says, "Honour thy father and thy mother." Perhaps you have wondered why the father is included here since the predominance of the mother in the family and home in our Christian culture is concerned with relationships to the children. The father and mother should share the responsibility of the home. A few years ago someone said, "This is a woman's world. When one is born into the world they ask 'How is the mother?' When a man gets married they say, 'What a beautiful bride.' When he dies, they ask, 'How much did he leave her?' From beginning to end it's a woman's world." But fortunately every man has had a mother and most men have had wives. And so God in his revelation has placed father and mother side by side in the text.

If we were to spend time searching the Old Testament we would find a great deal concerning the home, not just in the text which comes from the Ten Commandments delivered by God to Moses on Mt. Sinai. The whole framework of the nation of Israel as revealed and recorded in our Old Testament centered around two things. There was the tabernacle and later the Temple where God's presence was recognized in the worship of the people and the building stood in the midst of the nation to symbolize the presence of God among his people. In addition there is a tremendous amount of material in the Old Testament that exalts the importance of the family and the home. The Scripture places the responsibility of instruction and training of the children upon the parents, saying for example to the parents, "Train up a child in the way that he should go: and when he is old, he will not depart from it." Many commandments given throughout the book of Deuteronomy for example, deal directly with the instructional responsibility of parents.

Our text, however, fits in a unique position. As one studies the Ten Commandments as a whole, he finds that the first four deal directly with a man's relationship to God: "Thou shalt have no other gods before me. Thou shalt not make unto thee any graven images. . . . Thou shalt not take the name of the Lord thy God in vain. . . . Remember the sabbath day, to keep it holy." The latter five commandments have to do with man's relationship to his fellowman. Between these two groupings is a simple statement, "Honour thy father and thy mother." I think it is an outgrowth of one's right relationship to God. It is also foundational for a man's right relationship to his fellowman. The man who does not acknowledge his God will not likely honor his parents. The man who does rightly honor and worship God, and respects the Lord's Day will also be in a spiritual position to rightly acknowledge the place and the nature of the home and the family, and the authority of the parents. So these Ten Commandments are not isolated statements, but rather are interrelated one with another.

I think it significant that this Fifth Commandment has to do with home life. When we turn to the New Testament to see what it has to say about the Ten Commandments, we see that Jesus repeated the commandment to honor our fathers and mothers; and then he spoke about the ways in which people tried to escape that responsibility. The apostle Paul repeated this commandment and pointed out that it

is the first of the ten to add a promise, which related itself
to the covenant relationship of Israel with God in the Promised Land: that they would stay and live long in the Promised
Land, if they would honor their parents. To us this means
that a nation that disregards, and rejects the authority of
its adult citizens in the home is a nation that shall lose its
moorings and shall drift far from God and may lose its very
identity in the family of nations. Here then is a commandment
with a promise.

Let us look at the Commandment. First of all I would like
for us to look at the thought between the lines, if we might
phrase it that way, in regard to honoring father and mother.
Honoring father and mother perhaps is a presupposition.
Perhaps we could take it for granted but this is risky. Therefore, I must say that if we are to expect our children to honor
father and mother, father and mother must be honorable.
If parents are to be respected, they must be respectable. If
parents are to be trusted, they must be trustworthy. If they
are to be emulated, they must be exemplary in their conduct
and in their character.

One of the significant things about the nation of Israel,
to whom the Commandments were first given, is to be found
in the nature, experience, and position of their father, Abraham. Have you ever stopped to think about what Abraham
did? He is referred to in the Scripture as a man of faith and
a "friend of God." But what did Abraham really do? Oh,
we see in the Scriptures that his faith is spoken of in an
exemplary fashion because he left his homeland and went
to a land that he had never seen, crossed paths he had never
walked, created roads that had never been charted, knowing
only that God led him one day at a time. And we call this
faith. But when Abraham was walking out to a land that
he knew not, knowing only that God called, and God led,
there was something more underlying this that may be overlooked. Abraham was taking this journey because he had a
covenant with God, and this Promised Land toward which
he journeyed was to be the residing place of an unborn family.

It was to be the homeland of an unborn nation and all of this because of a covenant between Abraham and God. That covenant involved not just the land in which to dwell, but involved succeeding generations through which God would one day, at his own time and in his own way, bring into the world the Messiah, the Savior, which is Jesus Christ our Lord. The purpose God called Abraham was that he might have a family and through his family and succeeding generations he would be a blessing, the Scripture says, "to all nations."

Now then, I submit to you that the greatest thing that Abraham ever did was to become the father of Isaac. And all the promises of God to Israel were given on the condition, as you find in the Scripture, that God, who gave the promise, was the God of Abraham, Isaac, and Jacob. His family was his greatest honor, because his covenant with God involved the whole family. If you would look into the eighteenth chapter of Genesis you'll see that concerning Abraham God said, "I know him, and he shall command his children and they shall keep justice and judgment that God may carry out that which he promised to Abraham." Oh, the responsibility of parenthood. God entered into covenant with Abraham involving the redemption of a whole world. God entered into a covenant with Abraham including the coming of a Messiah centuries later, on the condition that God, in his foreknowledge, knew Abraham would be a good father. Can you see the implications of this? If you profess to be a Christian today, can you honestly say, "God saved me because he knew that I would not only be a Christian individual but that I would be a godly father of my children, and by virtue of this God could expect to bless the world through my children"? That's what he did for Abraham. He said, "I know Abraham. He will command his children and his children will keep justice and judgment so that I can carry out my covenant through them." Parents, did God save you in order that your soul might go to heaven or did he also save you in order that you might be the parents of a child that God could use in his plan of redemption for a lost world?

I cannot think of any greater honor that could come to Abraham than to be the father of Isaac. I cannot think of any greater honor that could come to a mother than to be the mother of a God-called missionary, preacher, deacon; an individual whose life is used and blessed of God as a channel of blessing to others. Oh, to be the mother or the father of a child like that. That's the greatest honor that could come and that was the honor and the glory of Abraham. I say to you today, that if a child is to be expected to honor father and mother, then the parents must be honorable.

A contrast of a negative example is found in the Old Testament. If you turn to 1 Samuel, you will find the record of God's priest by the name of Eli, whose sons were wicked sons. (I suppose some people have read 1 Samuel and thought that that was some sort of prophecy of what preacher's kids are supposed to be. But being a preacher's son and the father of three sons, let me hasten to say to you that any failure of character or conduct on the part of preacher's children is not due to inheritance—it's due to environment. Preacher's kids are what they are because they have to play with church member's kids! You can decide whether that statement has truth or value, at least it's an honest attempt at defense.)

Eli had two sons that were, I suppose, expected to follow him in the priesthood, for priesthood came by inheritance in those days. One night Samuel, the boy, was sleeping in the house of the priest where he had been left by his mother to be trained because she was giving him, "lending him," the Scripture says, to God. What a beautiful picture of a mother whose child was the son of promise, and the son of prayer, and that son, the Scripture says, was "lent to God." She left him with the priest to be brought up and prepared for the service of God as our families ought always to be lent to the teaching agency of God, that they might be brought up and prepared for the service of God. One night as the lad Samuel was asleep, God spoke to him and gave him a message, which he was to deliver to Eli. It was a sad and a painful task, this assignment that God gave him. God said to Samuel that night that the sons of Eli would not inherit the priesthood but rather the family of Eli would be cut off. Why? Because God said the sons of Eli had done evil and Eli "restrained them not." If there is a place in the Word of God, and there are many, that gives an answer to the permissiveness of parents this ought to be it. For the parent that "spares the rod spoils the child" and the parent that restrains not a child bent to evil is a parent whose own inheritance in the plan of God may be cut off. Certainly his honor is lost, his glory is gone, because he restrained not his children who were bent on evil. It is a sordid story of evil recorded in 1 Samuel about the sons of Eli. So with the contrast of Abraham and Eli, I point out to you that God expects parents to be honorable in their own character and in their relationship to their children.

Turning to the New Testament we see in 1 Timothy the third chapter, God's description of the requirements for preachers and deacons. Now, I'd like to say in their defense, God does not have a double standard. If you have any notion that you can do some things your preacher can't do, you'd better reread your Bible. There are some people that do things everyday of the week that would be shocked and horrified if the pastor did them, because "after all, you know, he's a preacher," they say. I want to say to you, God has but one standard. He expects his leaders, both preachers and deacons, and also other leaders of the churches, to have the responsibility of setting the pace and demonstrating the pattern for life. It doesn't mean that others are exonerated or turned free from responsibility—it means that somebody has to be first. The Bible says that before a man can be a preacher or a deacon he must "rule his own house well." He must discipline his children.

If I would tell the things that I have seen through my more than thirty years in the ministry that have disqualified men from being deacons, I would say that the lack of discipline of their children, even their conduct in the house of

God, is the most frequent failure. Oh, I know occasionally there is a deacon that has a moral lapse. Occasionally there is a preacher that has a moral lapse. There is occasionally one that falls below the high standards of honesty and moral purity, but for every one of these I believe there are a thousand men that don't know how to rule their houses well as a Christian father and husband. This is the requirement of the Scriptures. A man is to fulfill that requirement before he's ordained, not afterward. Churches should quit trying to act like seminaries to raise up deacons and preachers. The Scripture says, "Let them . . . first be proved." Let him prove himself in his home, as well as in his church life, then let him be set aside as an ordained leader.

While we are looking at these qualifications let me point out to you that the Scripture emphasizes that these leaders are examples. Therefore, the Scripture is saying by way of their example to every one of us that we, too, as parents, must rule our houses well and discipline our children. Abraham was chosen and used of God because God knew he would discipline his children. Eli was rejected of God because he failed to discipline his children. Permissive parents who lay down the bars and let their children do as they please, before the years of wise judgment, are themselves failing in their God-given purpose and privilege of parenthood.

Parental Responsibility

What a difference it would make in our nation today if all the parents that profess to be Christians would practice parental responsibility. There is a responsibility to be Christian parents, not only in our moral character and conduct but also to put Christian teaching into the hearts of our children in their tender years. God help the parents who accept the foolishness of the devil to say, "I'm not going to prejudice the mind of my child religiously. I'm going to let him grow up and choose for himself." If a cotton farmer did that, he knows that he would not reap cotton. Why should we do something for our children that will damn their souls

and destroy their lives that a man in his right mind wouldn't
do for his own field or his front yard. We spend more money
fertilizing the grass, and fertilizing the fields than we do in
planting the word of God in the hearts of our children. We
spend more time trying to cultivate and develop the productivity of our soil than we do in cultivating the character and
the ultimate productivity of our children's lives. Because we
put food on the table and clothing on their backs, we think
we have fulfilled our responsibility. Some of the ungodliness
that takes place in the lives of youths today—it may come
from a small percentage—but all the same, is a reproach to
America and is found in the records of juvenile delinquency
but should be charged at the door of delinquent parents. They
have been delinquent in their obligation to God, delinquent
in their religious obligation, delinquent in their moral obligation, delinquent in their parental obligation, delinquent in
their relationship to their children. Any child that grows up
making wrong choices has the expression of his own nature,
but remember the disciplining of that child is the responsibility of the parents.

In this day of ours when we have such an emphasis on
positive thinking, I would remind you that an author of some
of the most popular books on positive thinking has come out
with a sequel in which he says, "In this day we need to have
a positive 'no'." The parent that isn't able to say no to his
child needs somebody to discipline him. It is such a tragic
reality that we so steadily grow toward physical maturity
without ever having spiritual maturity, that some people grow
old without ever growing up. Consequently, some children
are all but damned to a devil's doom because they have godless
parents and weak-spined adults to live with. God help them,
for it is the responsibility of parents to discipline their children
and to show them by practice and precept, by lip and by
life, that which is right and acceptable in the sight of God.

Children's Responsibility

Jesus said there was no escaping the children's responsibility to the parents. Paul said the parents were responsible for the nurturing and upbringing of the children. He laid it to the responsibility of the fathers, specifically (Eph. 6:4).

Jesus spoke of children's responsibility to the parents. Perhaps we have not seen what Jesus looked upon, when some men who had the opportunity of caring for the needs of their parents said, "Well, I can't give them this money. I can't support them. I can't take care of their needs because what money I have has already been dedicated to God, and if you've made a vow to God you cannot break that vow." This was a tradition in which men could escape their responsibility by dedicating their money. Now it may be a fine point of technicality to say that if a man has made a vow to God he's obligated to keep that vow and to live up to it in the presence of God. This is true. This is scriptural. But in the traditions of the elders of the day of our Lord it had become a common interpretation and common practice that men tried to escape their responsibility to their parents. When they foresaw the arising of a need they would hasten themselves to the Temple and take a vow. Then on the basis of that hasty vow, they would be free of the duty to take care of their parents. Jesus said that is hypocrisy.

Children can honor their parents in more than one way. The first obligation of the child is to live such a life that he will be of honor to his parents. What a tragedy it is (and I've been there in the midst of falling tears, I've been there in midst of broken hearts, and tried so helplessly to console the parents) when the moment of information comes concerning the moral tragedies of their children. I say it is a terrible and a tragic thing when the life of a child becomes the shame of his parents. A parent ought always to have the right to proudly say, "This is my son." "This is my daughter." There have been studies made trying to determine why it is that in America where juvenile delinquency is so common, juvenile crime so tragic, certain ethnic groups do not have that problem. You can go, for example, to Chinatown in San Francisco and you will find little juvenile delinquency. Or you can go into Chinatown in New York City and you find little juvenile delinquency. Why? This has been the study of sociologists for a number of years; they have come up with only one answer to the question. There has been for generation after generation built into the very character of the Orientals the high regard for father and mother. The child seemingly has inbred within him the concept he would never say or do anything that would bring any reproach to the family name because of the effect it would have on the honorable parents.

Oh, if we could somehow build this into our children—that their first obligation is to preserve the family name in purity and honor. I know that this has been a consideration in my own family. I've seen some crises in my family's life when my father has gone to bat, as the expression goes, to defend the name of the family. I remember one occasion when a businessman in the community where my father had not lived long questioned his credit. Not because he hadn't paid his bills, but because the dear man didn't know. And when I went home and told my father that I had been refused credit in a certain office of the city, my father made no reply to me. He walked over to the telephone and called the man on the phone and informed him, "You do not question my credit, that is questioning my integrity, and for generations the integrity of the name of McBain has not been questioned and you shall not question it." Needless to say, when my father got through with him I went back down and got the credit. But that was my father's position. I believe that business would be better today if we could do it this way once again. What a travesty on justice, what a shame to integrity that a nation can fall away. And why blame it on the juveniles? It's the adults that have destroyed the honesty, the integrity, and the purity of family names. We should teach our children to honor parents by being honorable children.

There is also the responsibility of the children not only to honor their parents with their lives but to show honor and respect to their parents by obedience. In the context of Ephesians where Paul repeated this commandment he said,

"Children obey your parents, for this is right." This is right, "obey your parents." It is a tragic thing for parents to be found guilty of giving commands to their children that are not godly. We should never instruct our children to do something contrary to the Word of God. It would be a tragic thing, if a counselor of children should have to say to them, "You must do what is morally right in spite of your parents." It would be terrible to have to say to a young person, "This is the will of God and this is what the Bible says. You have to disregard your parents." For if parents are to be held responsible to God for teaching their children, children are responsible to God to obey their parents, "For this is right," saith the Word of God.

There is another passage of Scripture that has to do with mothers and families that may have material needs, and Paul in giving instruction to Timothy said concerning those families, "They should first learn piety at home." Children and families should not only have the mutual relationship of honor, and of respectability, and respect of commandments and obedience, but there needs to be in our homes that center of honor to God and to Christ where the family learns piety, and spiritual depth; where the will of God becomes supreme, where the Word of God is the authoritative answer to all questions and needs and purposes. This is the call of God, and we need today Christian homes built on such a basis as this.

The tranquillity and perpetuity of a nation are coupled with the keeping of this Commandment by the promise of God: "That thy days may be long upon the land which the Lord thy God giveth thee." And both the Commandment and the promise are repeated in the New Testament (Eph. 6:1-3).

5
Four Ways to Murder

Exodus 20:13; Matthew 5:21-24,38-48; 15:17-20

There are several passages of Scripture that deal with the commandment on murder. In the Bible, both Old and New Testament, God places a high evaluation upon the life of an individual. There isn't anything more important in this world as a person. This is often lost sight of because other values thrust themselves upon us. Some people set their goals in life on the accumulation of things, and they go out to get things, no matter what it costs. But this is not a Christian attitude. Jesus said, "A man's life consisteth not in the abundance of the things which he possesseth." God places the highest value upon the life of a person. This is one of the peculiar things about the revelation of our God. You can go into other areas and other civilizations of our world and you will find this quality is not there. Some cultures of our day have very little value on the life of a man. In some places it is a part of daily life to go in the morning and pick up the bodies of the people that have starved to death during the night. People think nothing of it because it's been that way for hundreds of years. Whereas in our culture we find some way of getting food to those that need it.

It has been a known fact stated by sociologists that one of the things that kept the population explosion from coming centuries ago was continuous war. Sociologists have evaluated the possibility of war between Red China and America and stated that if fought on the basis of manpower, China would win because she has more men than we have, and they are expendable in Chinese philosophy. Whereas, we try to find some mechanical way, some scientific way of fighting our wars and keeping our men out of battle, they don't. That is one reason why we are scientifically so much farther advanced than they are. A scientist stated some time ago in review of scientific history, that every major scientific development has come from the mind and life of a Christian, or of a man produced in a Christian culture. That is worth thinking about! The major developments of science have been for the benefit and blessing of mankind. No religion in human history has produced the high evaluation of human life as that produced by the revelation of God's Word, and this is the foundation of the commandment, "Thou shalt not kill." Nothing is so valuable as a man's life. Therefore, we must find ways of preserving life, at all cost. Preserve life as long as possible. It would be so easy in times of crises to "let nature take its course." But the health professions, our doctors, nurses, and their helpers are dedicated to the preservation of life and no one of them is going to cut short his own efforts and let a life ebb away because "the family is too large anyway." This is foreign to their thinking because our medical profession as you and I enjoy its blessings today is geared to the preservation of life. This is an outgrowth of our Christian religion. An evidence of this is that our hospitals are found in Christian lands or in lands where missionaries have gone with the gospel.

I often approach men who seem to have no interest in becoming Christians, and want no place in their life for the church—they would cross it all off—I just ask them, "Would you like to live in a land where the gospel has never been preached?" If you can find one you will find a place where there are no schools, you will find a place where there are no hospitals, and you'll find a place where human life is pretty cheap. These things that you and I take for granted today are by-products of Bible teaching. And one of the expressions

of it is, "Thou shalt not kill." It is not in the providence
of man by his own will to take the life of another—nor even
of himself. This is God's business. As I have looked at the
Scriptures I found four ways in which men are guilty of
murder.

Murder by Hand

The first and most obvious murder is by hand. That's when
you do it yourself. This is recorded in the Bible. We can
go back to the very beginning. The first record of the fruit
of sin was murder. Cain killed his brother over a religious
argument. They brought differing sacrifices to God, one the
fruit of his own hand the other a blood sacrifice according
to the command of God.

It surprises me that with all the methods men have used
for taxation to raise funds on the basis of legalizing the actions
of human perversion, they have not yet levied head tax on
murder. People who want to legalize gambling have told us
that we can control and discipline the gambling interest if
we sell them a license or charge a tax for the privilege. However, the cities where it has been tried have not proven it
so. They have told us that everybody is going to have the
liquor they want whether we like it or not, we might as well
legalize it and control it. Controlling liquor can be done by
taxing it and besides that, it puts money into the coffers
of the state. Taxing does not work.

The most obvious kind of murder is murder by the hand
of a man deliberately. With the premeditation of his heart,
he has gone out and taken the life of another man. With
his own hand, man has shed the blood of his fellowman. In
the Bible, God says, "Thou shalt not," therefore the man that
is guilty of shedding the blood of another man will stand
accountable before the judgment bar of God. As the Bible
says, "There is blood on his hands." It's not only true of
Cain, it has been true of men from homes on both sides of
the tracks. It has been true in the human race in cultures
and civilizations that have risen and fallen from that day

until this. Murder has always been with us in its very literal firsthanded commission, one man taking the life of another man.

Murder by Proxy

But murder is not always done firsthand. We find in the Bible that murder was sometimes committed by proxy. Now this, too, has been developed and commercialized by the crime syndicates of our nation, for a man knows when he breaks step with the gang that his life has a price on it. He knows that sooner or later his life is going to be taken. It is not uncommon to read in our newspaper of a man's death and they say that it was a "gangland slaying." What does that mean? It means that somehow it was an organized crime, somebody became expendable because he knew too much or did too little. For some reason he was a nuisance and somebody, perhaps by proxy, said "He's got to go."

The king of Israel sat in his elaborate palace one day. You remember the sordid story of the careless woman who could have lived twenty-five centuries later with her lack of modesty and lack of privacy. She took a public bath—and the king was enticed to sin, and one sin led to another sin. Consequently, King David called in the captain of his army and gave an order that the husband of the woman was to be put on the front line of battle the next morning so the enemy could wipe him out. We'll let the enemy wipe him out—"he's got to go, because I want his wife." David was guilty of murder by proxy! I think there is no one that has questioned David's guilt in the matter though David did not pick up the sword. David did not pick up the spear. David did not shed the blood of Uriah, but he was guilty of his death because he had another man do it for him. The men that did it didn't know that David wanted it done, but he arranged it and God did not hold him guiltless for that murder.

When it came time to build the Temple, David wanted to build the Temple for the glory of God. David sat one day, you will remember, (and this is something for us to think about) in that palatial palace of the king and looked out the window and saw in the distance the tabernacle, just a tent. And he said, "I dwell in a house of cedar, my God dwells in a tent." Right then he dedicated himself to the gathering of materials to build a house for God, because he felt in his heart that it was not right for him to live in a house more comfortable, more beautiful than the house of God. And in your heart you know he was right. The people of God from that day to this have looked at their houses and then looked at the house of God and said, "We need to do something to the house of God." But when he got the silver and the gold, and the things of brass to build the things of brass, and wood, for the things of wood, as the Scripture recounts, God wouldn't let him build it. He said, "You've got blood on your hands. Your son will build the Temple." David, the warrior, manipulated the armies at his own will, manipulated the army to slay a man deliberately, because he was expendable. David found himself faced by God, accused of murder though he did not kill a man.

The one time in the Scriptures that he was standing close enough that he could have slain his personal enemy he refused to do it. But on another occasion he did it by proxy. Murder by proxy. We need to be sure that as we manipulate our lives and plan the course of our lives that we do not do so to the hurt of other people. Although we might be able to piously say, "I didn't do it." No, but you made it possible for it to be done. It can be murder by proxy. It can be hurt of human life by proxy. Because we let somebody else do the dirty work for us, we are not thereby exonerated. There is such a thing as murder by proxy.

Murder by Heart

Coming over into the New Testament we find that Jesus spoke of murder in another frame when he said, "There is murder by heart." You may never spill a drop of another man's blood, you may never cause anybody to do so for you, but down deep in your heart you wish it would happen. So far as the judgment of God is concerned, you're guilty of murder. Murder by heart, because the passions of the human heart are the cause of murder.

Jesus said, "The defilement of a man is not in the washing of his hands," (as if to say it is not by the deeds of his hands either) the defilement of a man he said, comes from the heart. "Out of the heart proceed evil thoughts, murders, adulteries, fornications, thefts, false witness, blasphemies: these are the things that defile a man." That is the reason that Jesus spelled out the relationship of a man to his God in terms of his heart relationship.

A man is called upon to love his neighbor as himself. Jesus said, "They have said to you, to love your neighbor and hate your enemy." But Jesus would not place his approval on the hating of our enemies. He said we should love our enemies like we love our neighbors, and love our friends. You say, "Well, I speak to my friends and I speak to my neighbors but so and so over there, I'm not even going to speak to him." You better examine that heart of yours. If there is a human soul in this life, who is in this world that is not valued by you even to be worth speaking to, Jesus said, "Don't you even bring your offering to God until you are first reconciled to your brother." That money, you may call it a tithe if you like, but it is blood money if you try to worship God with it and at the same time are harboring hatred in your heart, holding grudges against people. Jesus said your sacrifice is unacceptable, therefore your worship is unacceptable. God will not accept it. Your prayers will not rise above your head. There is no sacrifice for your sins, there is no forgiveness, there is no song acceptable as praise of God from your lips unless your heart is right with God and your fellowman. He said, "Leave your offering there and first be reconciled to your brother."

In the midst of a worship service as we are preparing our hearts for worship through praising God in song and we come to the time of the giving of our tithes and offerings, it passes through your mind that there is someone that has something against you, you go then to that person to be reconciled. I wouldn't even wait for the sermon, God has already spoken. I would point out to you, Jesus did not say that if you have been holding something against your brother you go and confess it to him. Oh, I think that's involved, but he put it the other way around. The hated is supposed to seek the reconciliation. And so this pious answer, "Well, I haven't done anything wrong, if he doesn't want to speak to me that's his business," won't do. Jesus says it is your business, if you want to worship with a right relationship to God.

Murder by heart. When there is a grudge, when there is hatred of the heart, God holds you guilty of everything that that hatred produces, including bloodshed. You know, this is the shocking thing about our Lord. You see now why he said to the disciples in the Sermon on the Mount, "Except your righteousness shall exceed the righteousness of the scribes and Pharisees ye shall in no case enter into the kingdom." The Pharisee said, "I've never shed any blood, there's no blood on my hands." But what about his attitude toward the Gentiles?

When we stop to think about our attitudes, it has its modern applications. I grew up as a boy like other boys and I've seen some very bloody fights among boys on school grounds, in the streets, and elsewhere. I've seen some boys and a few girls stand around and urge them on and shout at them and encourage them, just as strong and loud as you do when you observe a football game out on the field; even though one of those boys may get up with blood all over his face and a broken nose. Some of the goody-goody little boys that have stood there and said, "Let him have it, Joe. Let him have it, Joe!" are just as guilty as if they stood there with a knife in their hands and let him have it in the ribs. They are just as guilty of spilling blood as the boy that pulled the switchblade.

Some of the racial riots and lynchings in our nation's history have taken place because of prejudice and hatred in individual hearts. Jesus teaches us that when we hate we are murderers in God's sight, as much as the actual killer. We have blood on our hands—every one of us, in the sight of God, it doesn't matter if some of us are preachers and church members! You cannot take God lightly when he talks about murder by heart. Jesus said that murder comes from the heart—not just from the hands. Some people in the holy name of religion have done things that ended in bloodshed. I believe in light of the Bible, God will not hold them guiltless until they come with honest repentance at the throne of God. It matters not whether it happens in Texas, Chicago, or in India. Murder is murder—somebody dies. Somebody whose precious life was worth the price of the blood of Christ on Calvary's cross. Who are you to say "let him die?"

In our hearts with our hatred we condone the world of murder. In our prejudice and in our blindness we allow the hatred and the passions of our hearts to give an amen, silent or audible, to the wrongdoings of men that end in the shedding of human blood. God help us! Murder by heart comes very close to the heart of America today. You and I need to examine ourselves very closely so our hands may be washed clean. Our hearts need to be washed also by the blood of Jesus Christ.

Murder by Consent

There is another way to be guilty of murder. Partially I have touched on it, but there is a shocking verse in the book of Hosea the prophet. In a day when religion had become corrupted he said, "As a troop of robbers, . . . the company of priests murder in the way by consent." In the book of Acts is recorded a tragic story of the wonderful Christian, a spirit-born, spirit-filled man of God, chosen by that first church to serve in the high office of deacon. Because he was filled with faith, wisdom, and the Holy Spirit of God, the Scripture says, he was chosen to serve. He was a godly man, a man with love and forgiveness in his heart even for those who stoned him to death. You see they tried to argue him down and the Scripture says, "They could not refute his argument." The seventh chapter of Acts says that when Stephen gave his defense they could not withstand him.

He knew the Lord and the Spirit of the Lord shone in his face. His face looked like that of an angel. As they stoned him to death, he looked up into heaven and saw his Savior standing on the right hand of the Father. In the language of our Lord he said, "Father, forgive them." The stoning was done with religious passion and hatred, with the pelting of stones upon the body of that wonderful deacon until he was dead and the pelting stones of his enemies covered his body. Standing on the edge of the crowd not raising a voice, there stood a very pious, religious, self-righteous young man, so separated, so detached from the whole thing as if he were too good to be involved and the Scripture says, "The witnesses laid down their clothes at a young man's feet, whose name was Saul" and it goes on to say, "and he was consenting unto his death." Saul of Tarsus was as guilty of the death of Stephen as if he had thrown every one of those stones personally. He stood there that day, not just as an individual, he stood there that day as a member of the Sanhedrin. He stood there that day with some authority. He could have stopped the whole thing, but he didn't. He didn't! He consented to it!

That same Saul, you will remember, had written authority from the chief priest to go to Damascus and to persecute the Christians there. It was on the road to Damascus that the Lord stopped him blind as a bat in the middle of the day, in the middle of the road. I believe that it was a conviction, a sense of guilt over the death of that righteous man Stephen, that made him aware that it was God that stopped him. Murder by consent. Hosea saw it when he saw, as the Scripture says, the "Lewdness of the day." Some of the self-righteousness of religious people is downright nauseating when we take such a self-righteous detached attitude as, "That's the way of the world and there's nothing we can do about it." We know full well there is something we can do about it.

You've heard the sordid story of the woman in New York who was murdered by a man who attacked her with a knife for a period of thirty minutes in the full view and knowledge of thirty-eight people who did nothing about it. They didn't even call the police. When her body was found and investigation was made, the people in the apartments around the area were questioned and they confessed that they knew what had gone on. When the investigating officer said, "Why didn't you call the police?" One of the dear neighbors said, "We didn't want to get involved." Yes, it's a sad day today because when you get involved you can be detained for hours trying to piece together a story for the police. The law of our land does not look out for the convenience of witnesses—it may for the justice of the guilty. But I want to say to you that there are thirty-nine people that will answer to God for the death of one woman because one man used the knife and thirty-eight of them gave their consent. They did not have a reason to hate. It wasn't murder by heart. They did not pay him to do it. It wasn't murder by proxy. They did not hold the knife. It was not murder by hand. They could have stopped it but didn't. It was murder by consent.

Christian people need to examine their hearts concerning their involvement in the welfare of other people. I would like, just in passing, to broaden this concept a little bit for you to point out to you the fact that today we are sending some people to an eternal devil's hell by consent. We could win them to the Lord, but we don't. We let them go on in their Christless, Godless way because we don't want to get involved. We have so many pretty little parties we'd rather go to. It may be that the priests of whom Hosea spoke, who gave consent in the way, were on their way to a meeting somewhere. By just passing by they gave their consent to what was going on. Much of the sin and the debauchery and the ungodliness that goes on in our society today is in the full knowledge of Christian people. Some of us are in positions of influence where we could change the course of human action and human history. But because of our philosophy

of noninvolvement, unconcern, and indifference we are consenting to all the debauchery, sin, and degradation of mankind, even murder, literally as well as eternally. We give our
consent when we simply stand passively, piously, self-
righteously on the sidelines and just let the world go by.

There is another verse of Scripture that asks a searching
question. It, too, comes from the Old Testament, but seemingly with a New Testament concern when it says, "Is it
nothing to you, all ye that pass by?" (Lam. 1:12). The writer
had described the suffering and the privations and the hard-
ships of mankind as people were hungry and naked and dying
and then he asked that searching question, "Is it nothing
to you, who pass by?" Oh, I've come across that verse and
it has rung in my ears like an ever living echo since the day
I first read it. Is it nothing to you who pass by?

It becomes an increasing wonder to me as I marvel at the
amazing grace of our God. There was Moses, who slew an
Egyptian with his own hand, guilty of murder by hand, yet
he found a place in God's grace; God used him mightily for
forty years. He was a murderer, saved and used by the grace
of God. There was David, who set up the situation and the
circumstances for murder by proxy and yet God said, "He's
a man after my own heart." By the grace of God he was
usable yet in the works of God. I find that Saul of Tarsus,
who consented to the stoning death of Stephen, was saved
by the amazing grace of God. And he was able to stand one
day before the ears and eyes of witnesses and say to them,
"I am free from the blood of all men." Such amazing grace
that God had forgiven him and cleansed him because he
repented of his sins. He dedicated his life never again to
consent to the death of a man; he dedicated his life to the
preservation of life and to the salvation of souls. With tears
he said, "I preached the gospel in the homes and in places
of public gatherings and I held back nothing that would be
a blessing to you; so I'm free of the blood of all men."

I had a privilege one day a number of years ago that I
will not soon forget. A deacon of one of the churches that

had been present for breakfast during a simultaneous revival had left to drive to his day's work. He turned his car around and came back just as I was walking out of the building with our evangelist. He came over to me and he said, "John, if you have a few minutes before you have to go I wish you would make a call with me." He said, "I just started to go to my office and as I was driving down the street I saw a man sitting on his front porch. He's an elderly man and I have been trying for years to win that man to Christ but somehow I've felt impressed that today is the day and I can't do it. I've tried so many times, and I just don't believe I can do it. I have to have some help." So my evangelist and I readily said, "Of course we'll go with you." So we got in his car, and we drove over to the house. There sat the old gentleman out on the front porch of his little cottage in his rocking chair. We got out of the car and walked up on to the porch. My friend introduced us, and we began to talk. We hadn't much more than passed the time of day when he said to the man, "We've come by to talk to you about Jesus. I've brought these two friends of mine. They're both preachers but I brought them with me because I want them to talk to you and I want you to listen to them. These men have what you need, and I'd like for you to know my Lord." We talked with him for a few minutes and explained to him how to become a Christian. The man said, with deep emotion, "I'd like very much to become a Christian but," and he stopped. Being the impetuous young preacher, I said, "But what?" He turned his eyes toward the door of the house that was standing open as he said, "But I'm a murderer, and my own wife in there doesn't know it. I never told her."

Then he began to tell us the story. Forty years before, back in the days of the livery stable, a drunken man started at him with a knife and, he said, "In self-defense, I reached down and picked up a neck yoke." He picked up and used the neck yoke off of a buggy to defend himself. As a result the man died. For forty years he had lived with guilt saying to himself, "I am a murderer. I killed a man." We tried to help him to see what God has to say and what society has to say about self-defense, but it didn't give him any peace of mind. Finally, I said, "Friend, do you realize that outside of the Lord himself the two greatest men in the Bible were murderers? And you can add a third to the list because one murdered by consent. Moses, David and Paul were the three greatest men in the Bible in spite of murder, because of the grace of God. What he's done for them he can do for you." He looked at me and said, "Do you mean that?" I said, "Yes sir, my God will save you now if you will ask him, believing that he will do it." And on that porch that morning four men got down on their knees, two preachers, a deacon, and a murderer. Four children of God got up from their knees and that man, nearing the three score and ten, with tears rolling down his cheeks, shook hands with each of the three of us and he said, "Men, it's all different now. I don't feel like I did before." That's what God can do for all sinners! Even for murderers.

While we realize the broad spread of Jesus' application on murder, let's remember that his grace is greater than our sins and our hope is in the amazing grace of Jesus Christ. What a wonderful message it is to those who may have a sense of guilt of any sort in their hearts. "Though your sins be as scarlet, they shall be as white as snow."

6
Three Kinds of Adultery

Exodus 20:14; Matthew 5:27-32; James 4:3-7

If I were writing the Bible I do not think I would have put the subject of adultery in because I do not like to talk about it. But one of the interesting things about our Bible is that in its divine inspiration God has not bypassed the facts of life. This is one of the things that makes the Word of God relevant and conversant with every generation. Every generation from the writing of the Bible until now has been able to look into the Scriptures and see themselves as if in a mirror. The danger, as James says, is that we will see ourselves and then as a foolish man we will go away from that mirror forgetting what manner of man we are.

The subject of adultery is not necessarily a popular one. Certainly Jesus' interpretation of this commandment is not a popular one. But all of the Scripture must be preached and all the Bible calls sin has to be condemned and from time to time has to be pointed out in order that we will not make any mistake as to whether it is right or wrong. Certain sins may become popular in society. Sometimes even in churches we tend to condone certain sins because of certain people. The Bible teaches us that we should not be respecters of persons and, therefore, I'm forced to the conclusion that sin is sin, no matter whose it is. Sin must be condemned in order that we might see the need for God's grace, and in order that we might understand the greatness of his love.

There are some dangers or occupational hazards you might say, in a preacher discussing the Ten Commandments, and I will mention one of those hazards. People sometimes get the impression that the preacher, because he preaches the laws and the commandments of the Scriptures and the demands of God, is setting himself up as a judge and that he is expecting or intending to determine who is guilty and who is not. This is not my intention. I am not a judge.

Sometimes we expect the preacher to be a judge. I remember one striking experience—I probably will never forget it. At the close of a Sunday morning service a deacon in a certain church came almost bouncing down the aisle to confront me with the accusation that I was preaching at him that morning. I said, "Yes, you and three hundred other people—what's your sin?" He said, "Do you mean to tell me that you would not write a sermon for one man?" I said, "I mean to tell you exactly that. I know where your office is and if all I have to talk about is your sin, I'll come over and talk to you about it privately. I'm not going to waste the time of three hundred other people while I'm doing it publicly." I don't think he believed me but he went on his way and I went on mine.

Regardless of which one of the commandments I am dealing with or even if I am dealing with other passages of Scripture that have bearing upon personal lives, I have found far more reaction from people who felt that God touched their hearts when I personally had absolutely no knowledge of the Lord dealing in their particular lives.

Then there was another humorous character in a pastorate who, when I seemed to get unusually close to him, would comment to me as he went out the door on Sunday morning, "Preacher, you sure let *them* have it today." And I suppose it may be that when one comes to preach on murder and adultery and stealing, we—most of us—might have the tendency to feel that, "he sure let them have it today," because we don't feel guilty of that sin.

There is a second hazard when discussing the Ten Commandments. Some people who do not expect the preacher to be a judge do expect him to be a policeman. Being a policeman is not his job either. It has been my unfortunate experience in previous pastorates to have been confronted with accusations concerning leaders in the church in regard to adultery and I was expected to do something about it. I never did, except when I was confronted with it sufficiently I would talk with the individuals involved in those cases, but at no time did I take it upon myself to discipline a church member because of his personal life—that's not my business. I'm not a policeman. I don't enforce the Ten Commandments. I just preach them.

Now in the New Testament we can find ample Scripture to indicate that it is the business of the church to discipline members from time to time. But it is not the business of the preacher to do it. If you have any reason to feel that any one of these Ten Commandments in the course of this study takes care of Brother So-and-So or Sister So-and-So, you better talk to the Lord about it and not the preacher. Because the Lord has a way of enforcing his own laws, and he doesn't often consult the preacher about it. This is one chapter I wish I didn't have to write but almighty God himself put it in the middle of the Ten Commandments and scattered it through the New Testament. There is no way for me to escape it and still be able to say with the apostle Paul at the end of the journey, "I am free from the blood of all men for I have not shunned to declare unto you all the counsel of God." Now let us seriously approach what God's Word has to say to our hearts.

Physical Adultery

There are at least three ways, according to the Scripture, an individual may be guilty of committing adultery. The first and most obvious one is envisioned in the first statement of the Commandment. The Old Testament has a great deal to say about this kind of adultery.

Let me introduce the subject of physical adultery by saying

this: God has a purpose for everything that he does. Our God is a God of order, not a god of confusion. As we looked at murder we started out realizing that the reason God forbids murder is because of the high value God places on individual life, and individual life is not to be taken by the hand of another. Here we find that God also places a continuing emphasis on the purity and the integrity of another. But not just the value of the person, all the way through the Bible from Genesis to Revelation, almighty God places high esteem and value upon marriage and the home. Don't overlook this. It is not that God is trying to restrict the pleasures of some self-indulgent men. Rather, God is trying to establish a home in which children have the right to grow up knowing that they are wanted, they are loved, and they have the security and mutual love of their parents which embraces the whole family.

God's high standards are reflected in the New Testament when God said through the apostle Paul concerning the leaders in the church, preachers and deacons, each is to be "the husband of one wife." Why? Because God says that his leaders are expected to be an example for him. Here again, we find another facet of the Christian home where the fidelity of husband and wife are involved. God sets a standard and says if you cannot produce a Christian home in which there is honor and true love, and purity and faithfulness, then you are not worthy to be set out front where the eyes of the world, as well as the eyes of the church can look at and follow you. God values the home. He says leaders are to have but one wife, and I am not of the school of the modernists who today are trying to interpret that to mean "one wife at a time." My sociology professor in college used to phrase it "progressive polygamy." (I don't think it's very progressive.) God was establishing the foundations of the home, and at the very heart of the nation of Israel was the home, the family.

God and Jesus pointed out that at the beginning God established his pattern when he made one man and one woman. Out of that he, and they together, grew a whole world.

There came a time when sin caused the destruction of our world, and God began all over again with one man and one woman and their family in the Ark. Again there came a time when God began to lay the foundation for the development of his plan for the redemption of a sinful, lost world. He began with a family. One man, one woman, and a child of promise. All the promises that have come to us as Christians have come through Abraham and Sarah and through the succeeding generations. The purity of marriage is spoken of with the strongest terms all the way through the Old Testament, even that they should not marry outside their faith. This is a point where Christians today are in grave danger because parents too easily give consent to the marriage of Christian children to non-Christians. It ought never to happen! Nothing but trouble can come. Even when there are two kinds of faith in one marriage there will be trouble. We need to have our marriage on a true Christian basis. The Bible says that Christians are "not to be unequally yoked together with unbelievers." This foundation is what God declares as the basis for the right kind of home, and it calls for absolute loyalty and fidelty of one man to one woman and vice versa.

The Old Testament text used the word *adultery*. In the New Testament, Jesus used the word *fornication*. They are very similar and in many instances seem to be used interchangeably. However, they are not exactly coextensive. Adultery in a strict sense of the term is the action of a married person in unfaithfulness to his or her marriage vow. Fornication, however, as the word was used in Bible times was a broader term that included even the engagement period and life before marriage. This was involved for example in the fear that came to the heart of Joseph when he first learned that Mary was expecting a child. You will notice the Scripture says he first thought he would put her away privately and avoid public announcement and embarrassment because of her unfaithfulness. Then God revealed to Joseph that this child was being born by the Holy Spirit and not by another man. Mary was only betrothed (engaged) to Joseph at this time.

It has always been God's plan that when a young man and a young woman come to stand together at the altar of marriage that they come in purity, having reserved themselves in every sense for each other. In the days of the New Testament being promiscuous before marriage was in itself grounds for divorce. If a man found that his bride had been unfaithful before marriage or if she found that her husband had been unfaithful before marriage, it was grounds for calling the wedding off.

According to statistics, if this were true today, 75 percent of the marriages performed could be called off before they ever take place. The statisticians have reported to us that 75 percent of the young people who stand at the marriage altar today anticipate nothing new in the experience of marriage as far as intimate relationship is concerned. What a tragedy and such a travesty of God's plan for human life.

God says, "Thou shalt not commit adultery." Jesus said that a man shall not put away his wife except for fornication (Matt. 5:32). There is no basis for divorce he says, but this one. Of course, today we can find all kinds of excuses to get around the laws. But the Bible teaches that a young man and a young woman are to keep themselves pure and reserve themselves for a true love that finds its fullest expression in the bonds and the experiences of marriage. There is no other setting for sex, except within the marriage bond and the marriage bond is a lasting thing—it is "till death do us part." God says, "What God hath joined together let not man put asunder." Jesus mentions only one reason for what we commonly refer to as a "scriptural divorce"; the physical act of adultery, which is unfaithfulness. Physical adultery is the failure to reserve the body for the purpose that God made it.

The apostle Paul in writing to the Corinthian Christians knew that they faced the problem of a pagan society where one little Christian congregation had been planted by conversion. Polygamy and adultery in that pagan society were major problems. It became a continuing problem, just as we have the problem today in our mission fields where polygamy has been practiced. Our mission churches require that a man find some way to resolve his polygamy problems before he is taken into the membership of the church. If he has more than one wife he has to find some way of providing for all of them before they will baptize him. They will not baptize a polygamist into a Baptist church on a mission field, because the Bible forbids it. I believe they are right in that kind of practice.

Paul found this kind of problem in Corinth. In 1 Corinthians 6 he said to them, "The body is not for fornication" (v. 13). He plainly said that the body of men and women was not made for sex, just as man was not made for the sabbath, but the sabbath for man. These things are not the purpose for which man was made. Paul says, "The body is not for fornication." This is not the purpose. License and freedom to do as we please in passing passions is not the Christian purpose for life, but rather we find that sex is a special sacred thing that is reserved for the significance of marriage within the framework of a Christian home and a Christian marriage. The man that steps aside from that is desecrating the natural abilities of his body as much as a man may desecrate the holy day of the Lord or a man can desecrate the power that is wholly of the Lord. A man can desecrate the physical abilities of his body by using them for purposes and intentions apart from the purpose God had in making him. That's what the Word of God has to say about adultery, and that's why it is sin.

Some licentious characters of the world would say, "God made us this way—he must have intended for us to act this way." This is not so. God did not make you that way for self-gratification because God did not make man to satisfy himself at any point. But he saw that it was not good for man to be alone. Man is not complete without that partner and that helpmeet that God provides for him. In this marriage bond and in the intimacy and unity of marriage man is made complete. Neither one finds fulfillment alone. One has no right to seek it elsewhere, for it is a debauchery of God's purpose and of the blessings that God has given to us.

So adultery, one kind of adultery, is the simple sin of using our bodies for self-satisfaction and destroying the purpose and the wholeness of marriage and all that goes with it.

Mental Adultery

We hear so many things, so many conflicting voices today. We have all read some of the articles concerning the morals on the college campuses of our nation. Think of what we expose our young people to. We hope that the Christian culture and convictions of Christian people preserve the purity and the Christian standards of our Christian campuses against these things so that we might have some refuge for our youth to avoid the areas where there is the licentiousness of a Christless culture. Out of the midst of this confusion, came the searching of a mother who wanted to find guidance as a mother for her daughters in the proper way of growing to maturity. She wrote an article that read almost with pathos until she revealed her concluding convictions. She said:

Most of the books I've dipped into deplore sexual experiment. They point out the physical dangers, the emotional involvement, the inconveniences and distresses of perfect passions, but not once did I come across a reference to right or wrong in regard to the greatest act of love. So what shall I tell my daughter about chastity before marriage. I shall be sensible and point out the social penalties attached to any other conduct. I shall touch on the possible pregnancy, the untidiness, the heartbreak, but I shall also say that love is never merely a biological act but one of the few miracles left on earth and if you use it cheaply it is sin.

And I say, amen. When you think of the lives that are lived by many young people today, apparently with blindness or ignorance on the part of their parents, it reminds you of what you see in stores where there is a bargain sale and you see some garment that has been marked down. You find out either by a little sign attached to it, or by close examination, that the reason for it being on sale is that it is "slightly soiled." Some of the cheapness that is attributed to marriage today, and some of the cheap jokes that you hear concerning marriage and the home are cheap for the simple reason that many of those who are approaching these sacred vows are themselves cheap, they are "slightly soiled," having been handled by many. I remember R. G. Lee once said, "Some girls seem to be like a block of salt, some boys may be like a block of salt—willing to be licked and mouthed by any old cow." With that kind of cheapness and the soiling of self you lose your self-respect.

The psychological and emotional damage done is keeping our psychiatrists and our mental hospitals busy today, to say nothing of the scars that are left on the soul of a man, the eternal soul of a being created in the image of God. No doubt we could say to ourselves "That admonition is wasted, I'm not guilty." A friend of mine went to preach one Sunday afternoon at an old folk's home a little distance from our college and he only had one sermon, apparently, so he let loose that afternoon on wearing shorts. When he got through that profound treatise, one of the dear old ladies came up to him and patted him on the back and said, "Young man, that was a good sermon, but you don't need to worry about us wearing shorts out here." I suppose some would console themselves in a Sunday congregation by thinking that we need not be worried about the sin of adultery as described in this Commandment. But I have news for you. Jesus had a few other things to say about it. Jesus said, "Ye have heard that it was said by them of old time, Thou shalt not commit adultery: but I say unto you, That whosoever looketh on a woman to lust after her hath committed adultery with her already in his heart." And I suppose that that verse of Scripture rightly read and understood would strike to the heart of every male member of the human society. I can not speak for the women. We need to realize that like murder, adultery comes from the heart. In the book of Matthew, Jesus enumerated adultery along with murder and lying as issues of the heart—the lust of the heart, the lust of the eye, the inordinate desires of the flesh. Though they may never be consummated in actual action, the intent and the unholy desire of a man or a woman is in itself a sin. Some people say, "Well, it's just as bad to think it as it is to say it. It's just as bad to think it as it is to do it, so you just as well do it." That isn't what he said.

"Plant a thought, you'll reap an act. If you plant an act, you'll reap a habit. Sow a habit, you reap a life. Sow a life and you reap an eternal consequence." Your future is dependent on where you've sown that life of yours, after the flesh or after the Spirit (Gal. 6:7-8).

The Scripture has much to say about those who live after the flesh; it is impossible to please God. In the flesh it's natural to have these desires, but Jesus said, "He that looks on a woman to lust after her has committed adultery already in his heart." He was talking, apparently, to a crowd of men, they didn't talk much in public to women in those days. But I want to say to you that the sin is no less because it's committed by one sex instead of the other. We need to recognize that the sin of adultery can be committed by the heart and the lust that is found within that heart of the individual.

Go back again and read the story of David. If he hadn't committed the sin of adultery, he would never have committed the sin of murder. He committed one to cover-up the other, and that happens so often in life. One sin leads to another. In that story, you will find that David did not make his decision concerning the wife of Uriah while sitting on his throne in his throne room. In an oriental climate where there wasn't any airconditioning, he went out to sit upon the sunporch of his house, which was on the roof where he could get the full benefit of the breeze. In a similar place was Uriah's wife taking a bath, cooling herself with water. David saw her and with the lust of the eye he committed the sin of adultery that resulted in a child being born out of wedlock, a woman being led into sin and a man into sin, a home ruined, and a man murdered. Such sorrow that comes, just from one so-called fleeting glance. I believe that we cannot read that story without recognizing that there was sin on both sides. Indiscretion, if you want to use the lesser term, for the dear lady on the roof. I believe that today some of the sin and the breakup of marriages and the high record we have in the United States of one divorce for every three marriages is a result of adultery.

Have you ever wondered why even sociologists who make no profession of religion are telling us that one of the great dangers facing America is the breakdown of the home? While we have an increase of church membership, we also have an increase of crime, until in most of the cities of our land women are not seen upon the streets even in daylight. I am just old-fashioned enough to believe that men are not entirely to blame, however. I think some of the indiscrete exposure of the female human flesh has something to do with the response in the indiscretion of male flesh. I remember one lady informed me, as the summer arrived, "Don't you ever call at my house without calling me on the phone first. When I'm at home I'm comfortable." And I said, "Lady, when you're at home you have a right to be comfortable, and I'll be glad to call you before I come." We got along quite well with that understanding all the time I was her pastor. I have often wished there were others who would have the same courtesy for the pastor. I don't even infer that everything that some Baptist preachers condemn in the way of dress should be condemned. I am simply saying that we have a problem on our hands. We have a nation today that seems to be more interested in reading pornography than a lot of other things. You don't have to buy it on the newsstand, you can see it walking down the street! You can decide which comes first, the chicken or the egg; the exposure or the adultery? The temptation is forever with us, and I believe that some of the sweet little girls that look so cute not in strapless gowns, but in gownless straps are being brought up with a seared conscience that knows little modesty. They are asking for heartache, trouble, and sorrow. Christians should have higher standards.

The teachings of our Lord make it abundantly clear that an adulterous heart can condemn a person without the evidence of overt action. This is a vital point to be found in the New Testament interpretation of the Commandments.

Spiritual Adultery

There is a third way in which we can commit adultery. We read it from James, "Ye adulterers and adulteresses," that's just the plain, unbiased word of the Scripture. He called them adulterers and adulteresses. He was writing to Christians. This is a surprise to some folks. I don't think he meant to accuse them of physical adultery nor of mental or moral adultery. I think he was talking about spiritual adultery.

In 2 Corinthians 11:2 Paul said, "I am jealous over you with godly jealousy: for I have espoused you [that's a good old English word for betrothal or engagement—committment] to one husband, that I may present you as a chaste [that's one who has practiced chastity] virgin to Christ." What was he talking about? He was talking about the faithfulness and the loyalty, the unfailing love and purity of an individual who has fallen in love with Jesus, and is found faithful to him. James is saying that friendship, flirting with the world, is adultery for a Christian because he has already been espoused to Jesus Christ. As a Christian there is a bond of love between that soul and his Savior, "Jesus, lover of my soul." It is not an unfamiliar reference that the Scripture makes concerning the relationship of Christians to Christ. Even the New Jerusalem is described as coming down from heaven "as a bride adorned for her husband." Can you see the beauty of that bride dressed in the white gown of purity and chastity, walking in simplicity and sincerity down the aisle to meet her husband-to-be at the altar, who is just as chaste and pure and as holy as she is. He says the meeting of the New Jerusalem that is populated by regenerated souls, as that city of saved souls meets the Savior, they come on the same ground of commitment, purity, and fidelity, as you expect a bride and groom to meet at the altar.

Paul wrote to those Christians in Corinth who were ena-moured by the world and still carrying with them some of the training of their previous paganism and heathenism and declared to them that they must leave all that behind, like the bride that leaves her father and mother and cleaves unto her husband—like the groom that leaves his father and mother and cleaves unto his wife. The Christian is expected to leave the world and cleave unto Christ alone. Any departure from that commitment as a Christian is as much a sin against Christ as a wife's physical adultery is a sin against her hus-band.

In all the worldliness of church members today, it's not often presented as adultery. The Bible teaches that world-liness of Christian people is infidelity, an unfaithfulness to their vows to Jesus Christ. Therefore, I should not flirt with the world, I should not have friendships with an unregen-erated world any more than I expect my wife to have flirta-tions or associations, indiscretion and otherwise, with men other than myself, or for me to have with women other than with her.

Becoming a Christian is a serious thing because you are making a commitment and taking a vow with Jesus Christ. One comes to the altar to say, "Till death do us part." But my friend, when you come to profess your faith in Christ and commit yourself to him as the Lord of your life, even death does not part you—it's for all eternity. "He belongs to me and I belong to him, not for the years of time alone, but for all eternity."

The reason that preachers, plead with you to be separated from the world and to be loyal and faithful to your church, and faithful and loyal to your Savior and Lord, is because there is as much expected of a Christian as is expected of a husband or a wife. As surely as our missionaries are not expected to baptize polygamists, neither are we expected to baptize people who have not separated themselves from the world. We are to be separated and dedicated unto Christ. Paul said, "I have espoused you unto one husband," and he said, he was jealous for them for that one husband.

A Sunday School teacher, preacher, or Christian friend may feel that in their Christian concern they have the right kind of love to talk with you about being faithful to Christ, just as your dearest friend might talk with you if he thinks you are reflecting upon the validity of your marriage vows. So your Christian friend might talk with you about your relationship to Christ and the church. It's one man and one woman in marriage, one man and "one Lord, one faith, and one baptism" in our Christian commitment and, therefore, we should have this kind of love for Christ that the hymn writer wrote of when he said, "My Jesus, I love Thee." Do you love him? Do you love him above all others, and above all other things? Do you really love him? Does he have first place in your heart? Does your faithfulness to him and his church demonstrate your love to him?

Paul made the comparison when he laid down side by side in his letter to the Ephesians the purity of marriage and the purity of Christian commitment. He said wives should be subject to their own husbands. He said that husbands ought to love their own wives, even as Christ loved the church and gave himself for it. Right in one context he talks about the mutual relationship of love and faithfulness of husband and wife and uses it as an illustration of how Christ loves the church and gave himself for it. A man ought also to love his wife because the two are one flesh, if he's unfaithful to his wife, he's unfaithful to his own flesh, he's unfaithful to himself. Paul used one relationship to illustrate the other, they are side by side, and to violate either one of them in either thought or act is a grave sin.

Jesus was confronted one day with a woman accused of being caught in the very act of adultery, and you remember the accusers left. I have thought of this so many times through the years when talebearers and gossipers have come to tell me what my church members are doing, no matter which one of the Ten Commandments they are breaking. Jesus said, "He that is without sin among you, let him cast the first stone." Let's not make any accusations, let's not be trying to take the little fleck out of another's eye when there may be a beam in our own. When he turned to that one lone sinner left there, the Lord forgave her right then and there and said, "Go, and sin no more." I feel that the love of the church may have to discipline. Church members some time or other may have to, as Paul said to the church in Corinth, "Put away from among yourselves that wicked person." Church discipline is scriptural, but remember that our Lord said we should at the same time be to him as to a heathen, and how are you to a heathen? The love of God in our hearts forever praying, forever loving, forever wooing, that we might win that soul to Jesus.

It matters not what a man's sin is. It matters not what a woman's sin is. It matters not whether it was daylight or dark if that one will repent of his sins and come to the Savior. Whether it's adultery or murder, lying, stealing, cheating, whatever, the amazing grace of God saves that soul right there when he comes. It's not for you and me to throw stones. It's for both you and me to forgive or take ourselves to God in prayer. For Jesus said that God forgives us according to the way we forgive others. If the sin of another offends you, pray for him, win him to the better ways and higher ways of the Lord. Don't knock him down, don't condemn him by stoning him to death. That was the Old Testament punishment for adultery and with the cold stones of heartless words men are still doing it.

Thank God for his amazing grace. Shall we love the Lord above all? He forgives every sinner that repents and trusts him, along with the cleansing power of his blood. Yes, the church is for sinners. I've had people ask me because of the known sin of their lives, "Would I be accepted at your church?" By the grace of God, yes, your sin is no worse than mine, and unless it's gone under the flood of the blood there's no hope for either of us, "By grace are ye saved."

7
Thou Shalt Not Steal

Exodus 20:15; Matthew 19:16-22

In Exodus 20:15 God says, "Thou shalt not steal." In Matthew 19:16-22 we find these verses:

One came and said unto him, Good Master, what good thing shall I do, that I may have eternal life? And he said unto him, Why callest thou me good? there is none good but one, that is, God: but if thou wilt enter into life, keep the commandments. He saith unto him, Which?

That was a very timely question because in the days of our Lord with the manifold interpretations of the elders and the Pharisees, they had many commandments. And for Jesus to say keep the commandments did not necessarily mean the Ten Commandments. So the man asked a very honest and sincere question when he asked which commandment. That could have been a question of desperation, because they had over six hundred binding restrictions that actually were interpretations of the Ten Commandments. So to say to a man your eternal life, your salvation depends on keeping the commandments, was a rather frightening statement. When he asked which one, Jesus said,

"Thou shalt do no murder, Thou shalt not commit adultery, Thou shalt not steal, Thou shalt not bear false witness, Honour thy father and thy mother: and, Thou shalt love thy neighbour as thyself."

What Is Stealing?

As we come to look at the question of stealing as discussed

91

in the New Testament, I think we could say that there are at least three ways to steal.

The most obvious and the one which most of us would include in our interpretation of the commandment from Exodus, is what might be called the denial of property rights. We may not have stopped to think about it if we have not been students of political philosophy, but actually our American system of private property ownership is of biblical origin. The right of ownership is something that is taught very plainly in both the Old Testament and the New Testament.

Now we find that both the Old Testament and the New recognized the tradition of passing by a field, and recognizing the ownership of the man that planted the seed and tilled the soil and all of that sort of thing, and knowing it was legally permissible for a man to gather food from that field and eat it on the spot, right there, as a matter of satisfying his hunger. But you were not permitted to put it into a vessel and carry it away. That was stealing. That was trying to take to yourself and store for yourself what another man had produced. But as a matter of preservation of life, a hungry man was permitted to eat out of another man's field. But even in this permission the Scripture recognized the right of ownership. Stealing then, first of all in its overt act, is a denial of property rights.

Property rights is an important thing and is the underlying point of our concept of "a man's home is his castle." Some of the rights that are declared in our Bill of Rights and our American Constitution are actually based on the biblical concept of property ownership. The authority of the law has no right to come into your home without a search warrant, because there is certain protection for a man's home since there is recognition of property rights. All of these things have been built into our democratic and free way of life under our American Constitution and are basically biblical concepts. Some of the things which we hold to in our so-called Christian America were established here because of the Christian convictions of our forefathers, who troubled themselves to leave those foreign shores and come to these and then to write into the documents of our heritage those things which the Bible says are the right of mankind by the right, authority, and sovereignty of God. Not the sovereignty of kings. So we have the concept that a "man's home is his castle." He has certain privileges because he holds title to a piece of ground; that's his home; that's his property. We need to preserve these things at all cost, not because they are our American heritage, but because they are our Christian heritage and recognize the integrity, the right, the privileges, and the freedoms of a man before his God, as well as in the eyes of his fellowman. To take these things from him is to take from him something which was given him by God, his inalienable God-given right, not just given to him by his government. Rather, the documents of our government declare these things to be recognized in our America. So stealing is, first of all, the denial of the rights of ownership.

Stealing is also spoken of in the Bible in another sense. Both in the Old Testament and the New we find some statements concerning the matter of dishonesty. You can steal from a man not only in the sense of taking from him that which he already claims but also in dishonest dealings. The Bible has something to say, for example, about using honest weights in business dealings. We have had a lot of jokes through the years about the old-fashioned butcher. If you read certain magazines you will find out that some of the principles of the old-fashioned butcher who sold his thumb every time he sold a steak really have not changed a whole lot. The only difference is you think you are paying for meat and you're probably paying for the label, the wrappings, and a few other things. This matter of honest weight is now enforced by the laws of our land, at least to a point where they have to test the scales. It is stealing when one uses dishonest weights in business deals by not giving a man what he has paid for. Now, it is not always a matter of meat, it could be a matter of anything that is being bought or sold. I have even seen signs advertising the dishonesty of dealers because I have seen them writing on a window glass that "It's a steal" at such and such a price. Well, an honest man wouldn't put it that way. What kind of advertising is that? You can steal it for so much. You can steal it for nothing if you wait till after dark, if that's what you want to do. When we come down to it, we find out that basically even in our philosophy of business today we still recognize the fact that stealing is getting more than what you should honestly expect. We can steal in various ways: whether we are stealing a man's money, or giving him less than his money's worth, or giving a man less money than what his product is worth. Dishonesty in business deals is stealing.

We find also that the Bible in the New Testament and the Old has some things to say about injustice in stealing. In the book of Exodus and in the book of James there is specific mention of the matter of wages and hours. The man that is being paid an hour's wage is expected to give an hour's work for that wage. And the man that expects to get an hour's work is expected to pay for an hour's work. James had some very strict things to say. A little surprising for his day really, when you look back to the fact that slavery was a common custom and practice. He spoke in very strict terms to Christian people about holding back the wages, and he wasn't talking about the withholding taxes either. He was talking about withholding from a man what was rightfully his, what he had earned. He knew he had earned it, and you knew he had earned it, but you didn't pay him. Taking advantage of a man because you hold the purse strings is stealing, because you have robbed him of some of the time, energy, and strength of his life.

One man may sell you an object. He may sell you wheat from his field, and you pay him so much for a bushel, and you are expected to pay an honest price for that grain. Another man may be selling you the very energy of his body, that is all he has to offer. He has no product but his own strength. He does not have any great skill to offer you and you can make his energy slavery or you can make it honest labor. We can steal by denying property rights, we can steal by dishonest dealings with measurements and prices, or we can steal in our use or misuse of mankind.

And I remind you again that through the Ten Commandments God is concerned about the worth of man. When he spoke of keeping the sabbath he was not concerned about the holiness of days, he was concerned about the sanctity of souls. He was not concerned about the worth of grain, or products, or days and hours. He was concerned about the worth of a man, the greatest and the highest of God's creation. And when a man underestimates another man's hourly wage, he is underestimating the worth of a man whose integrity is involved in the fact that he was created in the image of God. You cannot barter men like you do products because it makes a product out of a man. This is slavery where you buy and sell human flesh and it is injustice, and dishonesty. It is stealing; stealing a man's integrity. Just as by gossip you can steal his reputation, by dishonest dealings in wages and hours and products and productivity you can be stealing the worth of a man's life. We may be taking years of his life for nothing; this is as much stealing as taking bushels of grain from his field for nothing, or taking the title of the property for nothing.

In fact, I personally believe as I read the Scripture and understand the intent of God's will, the latter would be the worst of it all because the greatest values that God has placed on anything in this world is placed on a man. To steal a man, his integrity, his character, his reputation, his good name, to steal from a man what is rightfully himself, is the greatest sin of all. Some men are guilty of this. They condone it by saying, "Well, business is business." Yes, and dishonest business is dishonest business when it deals dishonestly with the worth of a man, and stealing is stealing when there are dishonest dealings with a man's property.

The Causes of Stealing

What causes these things? The Bible, I believe, sets out

three basic causes of stealing.

First, Paul tells us that "the love of money is the root of all evil." I suppose the love of money is one of the basic roots of stealing, dishonesty, injustice. Because when the man who loves money thinks he can materially profit he will pull any kind of a deal. You will remember that Jesus said, "Ye [man] cannot serve God and mammon" at the same time. So a man cheapens himself when he sells his own integrity for that kind of dealings. This love is really not love so much as it is lust, lust for the gathering of material possessions, when a man will sell his own integrity in order to get dishonestly from another that which is rightfully the others' and not his. Many times we have heard it said that Judas was not selling Jesus for thirty pieces of silver, he was selling himself. He was pricing himself. For thirty pieces of silver Judas would sell his best friend. That's not the value of the friend, that's the value of Judas, the value he placed on his own integrity and honor.

I believe when we come to this matter of stealing we are evaluating ourselves. What is the price a man would be willing to pay to become a thief? When we evaluate our business practices, our business principles where we are dealing with the worth of mankind and the worth of human strength and human integrity, human character and reputation, we are saying, "for so much I am willing to be a thief." There is the man that would not stoop to steal a dime from his employer but he would embezzle $1,000. He's willing to be a thief for $1,000 but not for a dime. That's the price he places on himself—that's what he's willing to be sold out for.

A man can carry this principle, I believe, right down to the point where Paul said, "The love [the lust] of money is the root of all evil." A man will do anything when he's willing to be sold for a price. Some people will commit murder for a price—for a price he's willing to become a murderer. Some people, for a price will commit adultery—for a price he's willing to become an adulterer. That's the price he places on his own character. The same thing is true at the point of stealing—for a price some men will become a thief. Some other men, because of the strength of their own character and because of the nature of their character as a Christian, will not be sold at any price. Basically, the first cause is the lust for wealth that will allow a man to become a thief.

There is another word that is used for stealing in the Old and New Testaments and that's the word *covetousness*. Covetousness is a cause for stealing and some might think it is *the* cause, but covetousness is a special word that demands special interpretation and there is a broader sense included than covetousness. Paul stated that "the love of money is the root of all evil," but certainly covetousness, the inordinate desire to get that which belongs to somebody else, is a basis for stealing.

There is another word, too, that is often overlooked and that is just sheer, plain, simple, old-fashioned laziness. Paul, in treating the question of stealing, said that man ought to cease to steal and go to work (Eph. 4:28). He put side by side the question whether a man is going to be a thief or an honest worker. So evidently, as we read between the lines at least, we can see that laziness is one reason, one cause for dishonesty and stealing. If a man can get it dishonestly, then he doesn't have to work for it. Laziness is the cause by which one man would seek to profit by another man's effort instead of his own. We should point out here, I think, that in the Bible we find the basic concept that God's people are a working people. I do not say that in a sense of class consciousness. I am not putting the management class against the laboring class as we speak of it sociologically. I am saying as a basic character of man, God's people are a working people, people who believe in giving an honest day's labor whether it's mental labor or physical labor or whatever type of labor. They're willing and believingly, honestly giving a day's labor for a day's wage. God's people are a working people. They believe in giving of themselves for what can be honestly earned. Whatever our skills, whether we think of it in terms of special talents or special training or special opportunities,

somehow we find a way to honestly earn that which meets
the needs of our lives and that of our loved ones. This is
Christian character, and there is something wrong with the
man that claims to be a Christian but will not give forth
an honest effort for what he thinks he needs for life. Laziness
leads to stealing—trying to get that which is not rightfully
yours (1 Tim. 5:8).

The Correction of Stealing

The correction is twofold. In Ephesians 4:28, Paul said,
"Let him that stole steal no more: but rather let him labour,
working with his hands the thing which is good, that he may
have to give to him that needeth." The Christian concept
is found here. As a Christian we cease to steal—that's something that belongs to the unregenerated man. So Paul is
saying that the correction for stealing is the conversion of
a man. Let him become a Christian. Let him cease to sin
by stealing, and let him labor with his hands that which
is good, for stealing is bad, morally bad. It is contrary to
the laws of God.

Notice the motivation for it. Not only does a man, as a
Christian, labor that he might provide for himself and the
needs of his own family, but Paul said, "That he may have
to give to him that needeth." A Christian labors not only
to get but a Christian labors to give. And, oh, how Christians
need to see this contrast.

There is that middle ground in which a non-Christian says,
"I pay my debts, and I stay out of jail. I'm a good fellow,
I ought to go to heaven. I'm honest." That's like trying to
live in a vacuum; that's trying to live in neutral. The worldly,
iniquitous, ungodly man may be a thief. Then there may
be that respectable man who makes an honest living. But
a Christian goes the second mile, he doesn't just labor in
order that he might honestly get. He labors that he might
give to those who have honest needs. A Christian doesn't
steal. A Christian goes to the opposite extreme—he gives. Peter
said that a Christian should not be ashamed for being a

Christian (1 Pet. 2:11-21), and a Christian should never be called a thief. You can rejoice when you're persecuted for being a Christian, but you have no reason for rejoicing if you are persecuted for what you have done wrong. Christians are to forsake these worldly things.

In Romans 13, the apostle Paul says that the secret to escaping all of these sins, enumerated by the commandments, is to have the love of God in your heart. The man that loves his neighbor will not kill him. He will not commit adultery, and he will not steal from a fellow man—not if he loves him. You don't steal from people you love. A Christian has the love of God in his heart, therefore, he gives to his neighbor and does not steal from him.

The answer to the problem is that we be saved by the grace of God and that we then seek to be filled with the Spirit of God and overflowing with the love of God, seeking to meet the needs of others in the pattern of the Master, our Savior.

8
The Unbridled Tongue

Exodus 20:16; Matthew 15:17-20; 19:16-20

The Topic of this chapter is taken from James (1:26), the text is taken from Exodus (20:16) and the context is taken from Matthew; so putting those together we have the Ninth Commandment in the New Testament. People have often asked Pastor Victor Ernest (author of *I Talked with Spirits*) questions about speaking in tongues. He says, "Why are you looking for other tongues when you haven't learned to control the one you have yet?" Now that may be a facetious answer for a serious question, but it keeps him from getting diverted from what he wants to talk about. But there is a bit of truth in it. Our tongues are quite often our problem. One of the things that our society always needs is honesty of speech.

As we look for this commandment in the New Testament, we find it in several places and in different words. We look again at the record of the young man that came to Jesus looking for a way of salvation, but like so many people he came with an attitude of self-righteousness, as if he had already earned salvation.

In our previous chapters we have dealt with other commandments including that of honesty, but honesty of speech is really a foundation stone of democracy. When you have the kind of freedoms that we enjoy in our country, even though year by year they become less and less—if they are to be enjoyed at all they will have to be enjoyed in the context of honest speech. As long as you have freedom of speech, it should always be recognized that it is freedom to speak the truth. Through all these years that we have had freedom of speech we have also had laws against slander and libel. And the Bible gives us additional laws against gossip.

False Witness

What is "false witness"? The most obvious definition is in a legal context because we associate the word witness with the courtroom scene where one gives testimony that may be dealing with the guilt or innocence of the accused. God has some rather strong things to say throughout the law concerning those who would bear false witness under oath. When there is false witness under oath, there is lying against God because you have taken the name of God in vain under oath. Normally the oath for honesty and truthfulness in the courtroom is done in the name of God. So to lie under oath is to lie against the name of God. This is offensive to him.

Lying under oath does something to you. Because whatever else lying does, it makes a liar out of you. That is harmful to your character, self-respect, and in time it will ruin your reputation. When a man becomes a liar dishonesty enters his character. If he accepts this within himself, then he is lowering his own standards and self-image. God is concerned at all times about people. Aside from what lying and false witness does to our Creator, it harms two other people. It harms you because you are the liar, and it also harms the person about whom we are speaking. These two things are sufficient reason for God to command that lying not be done.

Paul said, "The love of money is the root of all evil." We can take that statement from his letter to Timothy (1 Tim. 6:10) and go back and put it alongside every one of the Ten Commandments. The love of money and the greed for material wealth is often the price of bribery and perjury. It's desire for selfish gain that leads to a false witness, to a lying tongue.

Lying

It seems the wisdom that has been spoken many times
ought to be practiced more often. Whenever I come across
the statement, "If you can't say anything good don't say
anything," I'm reminded of a story that was told to me about
a woman. The story was about a woman who called a friend
to tell her something about a mutual acquaintance. She said,
"You know, I would never say anything about her unless
it was good, but sister is this good!" Gossip can sometimes
get too good not to tell. This is not the kind of good that
God is talking about. This is not the kind of good that simply
arouses your imagination or plants seeds in your thoughts
that lead to the destruction of a reputation. That is not what
is good. Good is what builds up a reputation, and what en-
courages, what emphasizes a good point of the character and
the personality of an individual. Proverbs 19:9 says, "A false
witness shall not be unpunished, and he that speaketh lies
shall perish." There is a sense in which we might try to make
a differentiation between false witness and lying. False witness
is under oath and lying is not. But a false witness under
oath is still lying. And so lying is lying with or without an
oath.

Jesus Christ put false witnessing in context along with other
things that are expressly condemned in the Scriptures. Liars
are in the same list as those who bear false witness, murderers,
adulterers, and thieves. Now many people who think themselves respected and honest in their business dealings, and
would never consider murder or adultery do sometimes play
loosely with the truth. The fact that Jesus put all of these
into one little verse reminds us that James said that when
you've broken one of the commandments, you are guilty of
them all. You see, it is not for us to say that breaking one
commandment is a greater sin than breaking another commandment. We are shocked with murder because it is the
spilling of blood and the irrevocable end of life. We are
shocked with adultery because we have been taught that it

is totally immoral. It destroys marriages, it destroys self-respect, and it hurts many people. But so does lying. Lies can lead to murder. Lying can lead to adultery. And lying often follows them both. Because the most common act for covering up sin is lying. When a person therefore, entertains the thought that lying is not as bad as other sins he is entertaining false thoughts, and he's using them for his own selfish purposes, and he is taking words and arranging them to suit himself, with no apparent appreciation for truth.

Jesus tells us that we will be held accountable for every idle word that we speak. Falsehoods can be expressed, as can any other communication, by the raising of the eyebrows, the expression of the face, the position of the body, the use of the hands. All of these things are part of communication. It is just as important for a speaker to know what to do with his hands as it is to know what to do with his mouth. Sometimes one's actions and speech do not coincide and that's falsehood. When one's life and words are not matched up we say this is hypocrisy. It may be a lying mouth but it may also be a lying life. We may be bearing a false witness by saying the right things, but with a contradicting expression on our face. Do we not sometimes very deliberately use irony and sarcasm, saying words but saying them in such a manner as to mean the exact opposite? Lying can be done in a lot of different ways. God says that false witness shall not go unpunished and the liar shall perish.

He wrote to the Ephesians and told them they should "put off . . . the old man . . . and . . . put on the new man which after God is created in righteousness and true holiness," talking about the regenerated man. When he describes the things that we should put off when we become Christians, he mentions specifically that we should put off lying and speak only truth with our neighbor. So you see the Christian is the one expected to become honest not only in speaking honestly, but in living his life in Christ he has the power. It is easier to speak honestly when you are honest. It is easier to act like a Christian, if you are one. But you can see that this is the answer to the commandment, "Thou shalt not bear false witness against your neighbor." He says to put off lying and speak truth with your neighbor. The difference between the two is the change that comes in a man's heart when he comes to know Jesus Christ.

In 1 Timothy 3 Paul says that deacons are not to be "doubletongued." And he says that deacons' wives are not to be "slanderers." And I repeat, I believe these are supposed to be examples, that means every Christian is suppose to have the same standard, to have the smoothness in their speech, and relationships with people. Paul is speaking figuratively when he says not to be doubletongued. At least in all these years I have never known anybody that had two tongues. Some people I thought might have had forked tongues, but I have never known any that had two tongues. What Paul is talking about are those people who speak two things depending on which group they are with. That's dishonesty. That's lying. That's being doubletongued. Also, using the tongue to be critical of somebody else, or to injure someone else, is slandering, which is expressly forbidden.

Gossiping

I remember when I went as a new pastor to a church some years ago, there was a man in that church who was supposed to be a preacher. Not long after I became pastor he came to me and said that he would like to come to my office and talk to me, that there were some things about the church that I ought to know. I told him, "You're free to come to my office anytime you want to, but if there are things about this church that I ought to know, I think God will let me know in time, and I'd rather not have them all unloaded at one time." I never did give him the opportunity to tell me what was wrong with the church. Maybe I should have because I was there seven years and never did find out, maybe God gave him an insight that he didn't give me. But I noticed that he was so frustrated about being unable to straighten me out on what was wrong that after a few months he became one of those that we commonly refer to as "inactive." He didn't come to church anymore.

I suppose there are those who quit church attendance because of frustration, but I am dedicated to frustrating the talebearers. I despise talebearing and tattling and gossiping with a passion. Paul evidently did, too. He mentions it in several places. He talks about whisperers in 2 Corinthians 12:20-21. Paul lived with a fear . . . can you imagine Paul being afraid of anything? I always thought he spoke rather fearlessly! His fear was that we are going to be disappointed in each other, but note, "Lest there be debates, envying, wraths, strifes, backbitings, whisperings, swellings, tumults: and lest, when I come again, my God will humble me among you." That's a rather ugly group for a whisperer to get linked with.

A preacher told me about a woman who came forward in a revival meeting in an old-fashioned church that had the old altar rail where people could come to kneel and pray. The preacher had preached on the tongue. This woman said, "Preacher, I want to put my tongue on the altar." He said, "Well, lady the altar is only twenty-nine feet long but you can try." There are some Christians whose tongues may not be forked or double but, may seem awfully long. I've told my boys the whole time they have been growing up that the Lord gave us two ears and one mouth, and that means we are suppose to listen twice as much as we talk. I think that is good advice to follow.

Hurting the Church

In a church that I pastored some years ago, there was a woman with a long tongue. She was bearing tales about one of the deacons. She might have been right, and telling the truth. To this day I don't know. But I visited with her. The policy in that church stated that any voice of complaint that might result in discipline would be presented in writing to the deacons before going before the church. She wasn't observing the policy. She hadn't announced it in a public meeting but it was sure getting to the public. I called on her and reminded her of what the constitution said. I gave her three choices. They were: (1) If you have the facts, put them in writing, and I'll take them to the deacon's meeting for you, because if they're true, we need to do something about them. (2) Secondly, you can shut up. (3) If not, I'll put it in writing and take it to the deacons with charges against you. The Bible has a whole lot more to say about gossipers than it does about women chasing deacons. Fortunately she chose the second. She shut up—she didn't even speak to me for weeks! But you see these things are serious because you hurt yourself. You get the reputation of being a liar, a talebearer, a gossiper. People hesitate to ask you to teach a Sunday School class, they hesitate to ask you to be in charge of a program, they hesitate to let you go out and visit prospects, they don't want you encouraging others to come to church because they don't know what in the world you are going to tell them. So you have hurt your own witness. They don't trust you with the truth, because they can't trust you with their own character.

Talebearing can also become hurtful because it can become the character of the church. There are churches that have reputations due to the activity of the members, they are the church, you know. If you have a few talebearers in the church, that soon gets around. Some people find out it isn't safe to join that church. You are exposing your character to gossipers, and it only takes about two of them for the community to conclude that the church is full of them. So you hurt the cause of Christ, you hurt the church. I believe that there is some kind of special condemnation that goes to those that hurt a church. 1 Corinthians 11 tells about some of the things that were going on in that church which caused people to "despise the church." Paul knew what that kind of language meant, because he was accused of persecuting Jesus Christ when all he had done was jail the members of the church. What you say about those who are the body of Christ, you are saying about Christ. The church is the body of Christ.

You cannot love Jesus Christ without loving his church because the Bible says, "The church is the body of Christ." When you gossip and slander, tell tales, whisper and talk about members of the church, you are inviting the judgment of almighty God. He is the final judge beyond whom there is no appeal.

The Cure—Bridle Your Tongue

I can sit down and spend hours in prayer and weeping with an alcoholic. I have by the grace of God led some murderers to God. I have sat down with adulterers and helped them mend their marriages and their lives. But I'll tell you, it takes a special grace of God for me to do anything but condemn a gossiper. I can do it, I have done it, but I would rather deal with a murderer, an alcoholic, or an adulterer any day than to deal with a gossiper. When you have dealt with a man who is in the chains and bonds of alcoholism, if you cannot help him, he is still what he was. You can deal with a murderer and try to help him and if you fail, he is still what he was. You can deal with an adulterer and if you fail, you are still what you are and so is he. But when you deal with a gossiper and if you fail to help him, you don't know what you are by the next morning. You may have the worst reputation in town, because anything you have said may be held against you. You are dealing with something that comes closer to being demonic than anything else I know of—the unbridled tongue. You better bridle it. And let it speak the gospel.

I want to close this chapter with a portion of the Word of God. Let it just sink deeply into your soul, and let God's Word say what it says, "My brethren, be not many masters [or teachers] knowing that we shall receive the greater condemnation. For in many things we offend all. If any man offend not in word, the same is a perfect man, and able also to bridle the whole body. [If you can bridle your tongue, you can bridle the whole body.] Behold, we put bits in the horses' mouths, that they may obey us; and we turn about their whole body. Behold also the ships, which though they be so great, and are driven of fierce winds, yet are they turned about with a very small helm, whithersoever the governors listeth. Even so the tongue is a little member, and boasteth great things. Behold, how great a matter a little fire kindleth! And the tongue is a fire, a world of iniquity: so is the tongue among our members, that it defileth the whole body, and setteth on fire the course of nature; and it is set on fire of hell. For every kind of beasts, and of birds, and of serpents, and of things in the sea, is tamed, and hath been tamed of mankind: But the tongue can no man tame; it is an unruly evil, full of deadly poison. Therewith bless we God, even the Father; and therewith curse we men, which are made after the similitude of God. Out of the same mouth proceedeth blessing and cursing. My brethren, these things ought not so to be" (James 3:1-10).

Let us not think that sin is only of the hands or feet; it is also of the tongue. If God has convicted you of your sin, you surrender that organ of your body, as well as your emotional, spiritual heart. Surrender yourself bodily to the lordship of Christ, to be forgiven of sins, to be cleansed and filled so you may be usable in the service of the Lord Jesus Christ.

So often we have sung "I Surrender All" in terms of all "things." I like to sing it in terms of all of me. All of my body, every member of it, all of my mind and heart, for we are to love the Lord our God with all our mind, heart, soul and strength. That includes our tongues. When we love the Lord this way, he will help us bridle our tongues.

9
Life Is Not Things

Exodus 20:17; Matthew 6:24-34

This last commandment is different in its relationship to the others. In its original form it was the only one that dealt with the desire instead of the overt act. Most of the commandments, therefore, are dealing with the actions either that men perform in relationship to God or to their fellowman. This one, however comes directly to the problem of the heart because it speaks of covetousness, which is a condition and an attitude of the heart.

Covetousness Causes All Kinds of Evil

The apostle Paul stated, "The love of money is the root of all evil" (1 Tim. 6:10). Actually he said two things for us to notice. First of all, notice the fact that the word "all" in this verse means all kinds of evil, not necessarily every individual act of evil. The second thing to note is that he's speaking of the *love* of money. Money is not the root of all kinds of evil but the *love* of money is the root of all kinds of evil.

A third thought should perhaps be drawn here, and that is that this word *money* may be used in something of a symbolic sense in that it is not speaking of money in the literal sense of a coin or currency but in terms of a symbol of personal gain. This is what brings us to the concept of covetousness as forbidden in this Tenth Commandment.

The First Commandment has to deal with the one true

God. Job said, "If I have made gold my hope, . . . I should have denied the God that is above" (Job 31:24,28). Making gold his hope, and material gain his single goal in life is what man has always had to struggle against. Job said rightly and wisely, "If I have done this then I have denied God." Jesus said man cannot serve two masters (Matt. 6:24). We cannot love, worship, and become subservient to the demands of both materialism and God. Covetousness is that inner desire of material things and particularly those things that belong to another. As the commandment tells us, we are not to covet a man's possessions, not even his wife or his servants. Jesus said this kind of thing becomes the master of life, and when you are serving this master you cannot serve God. Therefore, covetousness breaks the First Commandment.

The Second Commandment deals with idolatry. We are told in the Scripture by the apostle Paul, (Eph. 5:5 and Col. 3:5) "Covetousness is idolatry." This is twice stated which should stress to us that the very attitude of covetousness, the heart condition of covetousness, is in itself an overt act of idolatry. We become a worshiper of money. And so some of the evils that are associated with idolatry are initiated and implemented and motivated by covetousness.

The Third Commandment deals with profanity. Profanity is taking God's name in vain. The story of Ananias and Sapphira gives us an example of how people will make false promises in the name of God in order to gain pride and recognition in the eyes of men, and at the same time keep for themselves those material things which they are pledging to give to someone else. In this passage Peter made it clear to Ananias and Sapphira that they had made a covenant to the Holy Spirit not just to man. They had made a promise to a church. They had made a commitment in the presence of the apostles. But he said, "You lied to God." In this kind of evil we are taking God's name in vain, and there is no way to explain it except with the word covetousness.

The Fourth Commandment has to do with the sabbath. How often is the piety, the sanctity, the holiness of the Lord's

Day violated because of covetousness, the love of money. We are living in an industrial age. Some of us today can remember when businesses were closed on Sunday. We can remember the trauma of this nation when under the pressure of war we found the industries working twenty-four hours a day, seven days a week. But when the war was over, we never did go back to the recognition of the Lord's Day as a day of rest as it had been before, because businessmen found out they could make more profit in seven days than they could in six. The welfare of the worker, the welfare of society, the welfare of a nation had been sacrificed by the industrialists because of profits on the Lord's Day. This situation is not all management's fault, however, because many working people prefer to work on Sunday since they get time and a half on Sunday, or they can get another day's work in on Sunday. So whatever a man's position or place in society we have seen the society of America shift to a seven-day-a-week concept with stores open, businesses open and industry going full speed ahead seven days a week for no other reason than the profit motive. Now the profit motive has done a lot of good in our world. It has caused scientific breakthroughs, it has caused unmeasurable developments for the welfare of man. But when it has come in the form of sheer covetousness, it has become a degrading thing that has broken down the spirituality of a people, because it has destroyed the proper recognition of the sabbath as a day of rest and a day of worship.

The Fifth Commandment has to do with the honoring of our fathers and our mothers. Jesus gave an example (Matt. 15:1-6) of those who made religious commitments in order to avoid fulfilling their obligation to their parents in the way of personal support. Then when the parents asked for some of the material possessions of their children for the support of life, they said, "It has been dedicated as a gift to God." Here is an example from our Lord of some people who because of covetousness had broken the Fifth Commandment and had failed to show proper honor to their mother and father. The fact that it was done under the guise of religion and religious covenants and vows makes it even worse. Many parents have wept when the family honor was lost because of sin in the children, due to covetousness. Children should bring pride and honor and glory to their parents, but parents have no reason to be proud of cold, materialistic children who get ahead materially in the world but who shrivel spiritually.

The Sixth Commandment says, "Thou shall not kill." What kind of murder has not been perpetrated by covetousness? Men have killed to get. Even David was guilty of murder because he wanted a man's wife for himself. Others have killed because they wanted a man's field, such as King Ahab and Queen Jezebel, and through the centuries have taken the life of men in order to get without opposition what belonged to another. Even in the supreme case of Judas, he sold Jesus to the cross for a dollar and a half.

The Seventh Commandment deals with adultery. Thousands of women enter white slavery every year because they have coveted the gains that can come from it, and they earn money for their masters and they earn a livelihood for themselves. Adultery in that case is caused by the love of money. Prostitution is a business, and both women and men have sold their bodies into the sin of adultery for what they can get from it. Business men provide prostitutes as part of business deals in order to get a better deal. This kind of thing goes on in American society as well as in other parts of the world continually. How many men have committed adultery because they have coveted their neighbor's wife? This is at the heart of it all.

The Eighth Commandment says, "Thou shall not steal." There's certainly no difficulty relating covetousness and stealing. One classic example is found in the seventh chapter of Joshua where Achan answered Joshua's examining questions and said, "I have indeed sinned against the Lord God of Israel, and thus and thus have I done: When I saw among the spoils a goodly Babylonish garment and two hundred shekels of silver, and a wedge of gold of fifty shekels weight, then *I coveted them, and took them*" (Josh. 7:20-21). All through the history of mankind men's eyes have drawn them into sin, because we have seen and we have lusted. We have coveted, whether it be things or people. And these feelings of covetousness have motivated men to steal, to take what did not belong to them, whether it was picking up a small coin or stealing an automobile or shoplifting in the grocery stores. All of these things come out of covetousness. All kinds of stealing can be motivated by covetousness.

The Ninth Commandment deals with false witness. Many false witnesses have been bribed for money. All through the Bible we have records of those who gave a false witness because they were paid to do so. Even the soldiers that guarded the tomb lied and said the body of Jesus was stolen instead of resurrected. These soldiers met with the elders in Israel and reported to them what had happened at the tomb. The Scripture records in Matthew 28:12 that the elders gave the soldiers a large sum of money so that they would say that the apostles came by night and stole Christ's body away while they slept.

Bribery of public officials is still with us in government and society. Men and women have been lying for all of human history in order to get what was not rightfully theirs. This is the way in which covetousness becomes the root of false witness and, therefore, contributes and motivates a person to break the Ninth Commandment.

The Tenth Commandment of course is the commandment on covetousness. Covetousness is a wicked cancer of the heart cured only by the saving grace of God.

Life Is Not Things

Jesus said, "A man's life consisteth not in the abundance of the things which he possesseth" (Luke 12:15). This is where we learn that covetousness hurts ourselves. Some say that Christianity is opposed to wealth, that you can not be a wealthy man and be a Christian at the same time. This is not the teachings of the Scriptures. But the teachings of Jesus

Christ bring out to us that a man's life and a man's possessions
are two different things. Christianity is not opposed to riches.
It is opposed to worshiping riches. It is opposed to dishonest
riches. Jesus taught that we should use riches for the honor
and glory of God.

One of the dangers of covetousness in our lives is that it
gives us a false standard of living. We are not suppose to
be living in competition with or envy of our fellowman. Competition in business may be healthy but covetousness can
motivate a dishonest competition. Covetousness can motivate
an unfair competition. When it does, it makes something
dishonest and something unfair out of us. Our lives therefore,
consist of something more valuable, more spiritual, and more
eternal than the things that we may gain by the operation
of our lives. Our standard of living must be determined by
honest gains and by spiritual values.

Remember the Word of God teaches, "Man does not live
by bread alone, but by every word that proceedeth out of
the mouth of God" (Deut. 8:3; Matt. 4:4). When we think
in terms of our standard of living, it is easy for covetousness
to direct a life in the way of the philosophy that says "after
all I have to eat," or it says, "after all I have to live." Man
does not have to eat and man does not have to live. He could
die, and it would be better to die honestly than to live dishonestly. It is better to die morally right and honorable than
to live immorally. Man's life consists of an inner image of
God. Man's life consists of a soul, a spiritual entity that is
capable of fellowship and cooperation and identification with
God. Bread does not necessarily contribute to this. Things
do not necessarily contribute to this. If we make these things
the object and the passion of our lives, then we are getting
into idolatry instead of true worship and man's philosophy
becomes materialistic; he forgets that life is not things.

I stated that Christianity is not opposed to riches. Let me
pose another question. How rich then, can a Christian be?
The story has been repeated that Dr. B. H. Carroll asked
his Sunday School class this question, "What New Testament

Scripture shows how much money a man may lawfully acquire?" He posed the question on a Sunday morning as an appetizer for the lesson the following Sunday. A wealthy man who was attending that day came to him at the close of the session and said, "I will not be able to be present next Sunday. I'll be out of the city on business. But I must know your answer to that question." This man made a fortune in Texas and became a philanthropist. The answer that he found from Dr. B. H. Carroll is recorded in 3 John 2. John was apparently writing to a wealthy man, and gave this word of blessing when he said, "Beloved, I wish above all things that thou mayest prosper and be in health, even as thy soul prospereth." This tells us how rich a man can be as a Christian. It says that one should prosper materially as long as his material prosperity does not exceed his spiritual prosperity.

If a man then sacrifices the Lord's Day in order to make money, he is decreasing his spiritual prosperity in order to increase his material prosperity. This is a violation of the prayer of admonition of John. You can take this principle into almost any area of the use of time or things, or life, or people, and keep in mind that life is spirit because life is of God. A Christian created in the image of God and regenerated in the likeness of Jesus Christ, is then to keep his life physically and materially subjected to the dominance of the Holy Spirit of God. This demands that he give first concern to the spirit and that he not allow his material prosperity to excel or exceed his spiritual prosperity.

Dr. Carroll went on to say, "If you have moved from a cottage to a palace and your soul no longer prospers, you had better move back to the cottage." If we covet and get, we lose our own spiritual lives. Jesus asked, "What is a man profited, if he shall gain the whole world, and lose his own soul?" (Matt. 16:26).

What Should We Covet?

God's Word makes it very plain that one cannot covet

material things and have a spiritual priority in his life. Man cannot serve both God and mammon. In the Old Testament God prescribed a jubilee. This was God's plan for returning the land to its original owner at fifty year intervals. This helped to curb covetousness.

Paul tells us (1 Tim. 6:7), "We brought nothing into this world, and it is certain we can carry nothing out." It is important for us to see then that both the Old Testament and the New show the handiwork of God in trying to place man in such a way that his life would be directed in spiritual pursuits and not become captivated and enslaved by material things. If a man knows and remembers daily that those material things which he possesses shall one day slip from his hands like sand through the fingers, that he will someday no longer be able to grasp and to grip the things of this world, it will help him realize that he must then search and reach for things of the spirit and things that last for eternity. Covetousness describes the man's grasping for things of this world.

Paul tells us "While we look not at the things which are seen, but at the things which are not seen; for the things which are seen are temporal; and the things which are not seen are eternal" (2 Cor. 4:18). Man in his physical existence naturally places value on the things that he sees. He even finds it difficult to envision a God who is spirit and not body and, therefore, he has created idols as objects of worship. Man has found it difficult to envision things being of worth which he cannot hold in his hand. How do you grasp love? How do you grasp truth? How do you embrace righteousness? You do not do it with the hands of your body. Man must, therefore, continually be told again and again that he must seek that which is unseen and not that which is seen. The things which we see are things which we can earn, things which we can build, things which we can fashion with our hands, things which we can grasp in this world. These are not things that we brought into the world with us. They were already here in one form or another and when we leave this world they will still be here in one form or another. We brought nothing into the world, and we will take nothing out of the world.

The story is recorded that Alexander the Great requested that holes be cut in his coffin so his hands could be extended for all to see that the king of the world was taking nothing with him.

Some years ago I made the statement to a group of women, "There are no pockets in shrouds—you cannot take it with you." One woman spoke up and said, "There'll be a pocket in my shroud because I'm going to sew it in ahead of time." Her attitude seemed to be, "If I can't take it with me, I'm not going." The fact of life is we are all going and leaving everything on this earth behind.

Life is sometimes described in various ways in relationship to material things. Some people's whole lives are involved in getting. This decreases our own real value. Someone has said, "We too often love things and use people, instead of loving people and using things." We even use and abuse ourselves as tools to get things. This is often motivated by covetousness and a materialistic concept of success. Success is too often measured by dollars. Many times in evaluating our childhood, we speak of it in terms of affluence or being deprived. Youth are often encouraged by counselors to get an education because it increases their earning power.

I pastored for a number of years in the state of Missouri. For many years in Chillicothe, Missouri, there was a business college which advertised all over the country with signs that said, "Learn more to earn more." This is an unworthy motive for education. Education should do something, besides giving a person an increased earning power. When we evaluate the life of adults, we ask such questions as how much does he earn? How much does he have? When death comes we say, "How much did he leave?" Fact of the matter is he left it all.

There is a story often quoted of a Scotsman who died. A friend inquired, "How much did he leave?" Another who knew him well said, "He didn't leave anything. God took him away from it." This describes too many people for the welfare of our society.

Coming back to the context of our New Testament text (1 Tim. 6:9-10), Paul said, "They that will be rich fall into temptation and a snare, and into many foolish and hurtful lusts, which drown men in destruction and perdition. For the love of money is the root of all evil: which while some coveted after, they have erred from the faith, and pierced themselves through with many sorrows."

Covetousness leads men away from the faith and brings spiritual destruction to their lives, and they can lose their Christian witness easily. In Galatians the apostle Paul sets it out for us in clear contrast so that we can see the direction of our lives, "Be not deceived; God is not mocked: for whatsoever a man soweth, that shall he also reap. For he that soweth to his flesh shall of the flesh reap corruption; but he that soweth to the Spirit shall of the Spirit reap life everlasting" (Gal. 6:7-8).

Covetousness is setting the direction of our lives toward material things. These things shall return to dust and the man who sows and invests his life in material things shall have the same end. Spiritual things are for eternity and he who sows or invests his life in these things shall have been wise.

One form of Christian covetousness is found in 1 Corinthians 12:31, when Paul said, "But covet earnestly the best gifts: and yet show I unto you a more excellent way." Even in the spiritual realm there are choices to be made. Some things excel other things. Paul gave to us the challenge in principle, the Christian needs to covet the better things. As a Christian I should seek the better gifts for a greater service for my Lord. As a Christian I must invest my life in better pursuits, reaching for spiritual goals until the very character of those goals becomes the character of my life. The man that is honest is the man who strives for honesty. The man who is pure is the man who strives for purity. The man who is lovable is the man who strives to love. The man who is righteous is the man who strives to be right. The man who is godly is the man who strives to be like God. These things then characterize Christian covetousness. They do not break the Tenth Commandment, but they build Christian character that would be acceptable in the presence of God. For we are to be conformed to the image of his Son. This goal should be what Christians strive for and then this goal will become the character of our lives.